EASTER IDEA BOOK

This book, the first of its kind, brings information and inspiration to all those homemakers who are today making Easter second only to Christmas as a time for family gathering and gift-giving, and a season for joyous, friendly entertaining, following the somber days of Lent.

In Part I. *Easter Food and Parties,* however, the author also offers interesting dishes for fast days. Then she gives recipes, menus, decorating ideas, even children's games, for the day of celebration and the welcome spring weeks that follow. Here are the 8 stimulating chapters: *Lenten Dishes Come First — All About Ham — Easter Cakes and Breads — Easter Breakfasts and Luncheons — Easter-Day Dinners and Afternoon Parties — Parties for Children — Easter Eggs to Dye or Make — Centerpieces and Favors.*

Part II. *Easter Gifts,* gives detailed directions for amusing and useful gifts you can sew, crochet, tat, or paint from an Easter greeting card to a bunny suit for your youngest or a pair of socks for the man in your life. The future of azalea, lily, and hydrangea left in your probably helpless hands is also carefully explained. Here are 5 chapters with a multitude of brand new ideas on: *Easter Baskets — About Easter Pets — Gifts to Make for Children — Gifts to Make for Adults — Easter Cards and Easter Plants.*

Written for all who want to make the spring festival at home, as well as at church, a specially lovely and memorable occasion, the *Easter Idea Book* is in every way true to its name.

FRONTISPIECE – EASTER DINNER

EASTER
IDEA BOOK

By Charlotte Adams

M. BARROWS AND COMPANY, INCORPORATED

PUBLISHERS, NEW YORK

For
Helen Lindholm
with love and gratitude

Copyright 1954 by Charlotte Adams
Library of Congress Catalog Card Number 54-5378
Manufactured in the United States of America
First Printing   1954

Contents

My great appreciation goes to Frances Barton of General Foods; Martha Logan of Swift and Company; Betty Crocker of General Mills, Inc.; The Ralston Purina Company; The Dennison Manufacturing Company; The Spool Cotton Company; The American Thread Company; and Botany Mills for the help they have given me with this book.

Illustrations

(D R A W I N G S)

Part I

EASTER FOOD AND PARTIES

We Celebrate Easter

Easter is the season of promise and hope and new life. Even though it has stood for over fifteen hundred years as the symbol of the resurrection of Jesus to members of the Christian Church, it is not entirely a Christian festival. Its origins go far back into pagan rites and customs. All of them are influenced by men's hope and belief in rebirth. Every spring up from the ground and out of bare branches come nature's illustrations of that rebirth.

No matter what our individual backgrounds, Easter is a season of joy and each of us wants to celebrate it in a spirit of love and kindness and pleasure in new life emerging from darkness or even death.

Aside from its deep religious connotations, there are other symbols of Easter which become familiar to us as children and many of which undoubtedly date back to a primitive past. The egg, for instance—how did it become identified with Easter? There are many theories but nobody really knows. Ancient mythology relates the egg to the beginnings of life—and of the world. A connection can easily be thought out between the emergence of the world from original chaos and the emergence of Christ from the tomb. So this may be how the symbol of an egg became connected with Easter.

It is thought that perhaps the custom of coloring eggs and decorating them elaborately may have been brought back to Europe by warriors in the crusades. In any event, these customs are certainly strongly with us now, and dear to the heart of every child—big or little.

How, in our modern American version, the egg got to be identified with a rabbit instead of a hen is also something of a puzzle. I lean to the opinion that the rabbit's obvious identification with fertility may have brought him into the Easter picture. But why he is responsible for Easter eggs is still a mystery.

Lambs are certainly typical Easter symbols and doubtless are so because the Hebrew Paschal Lamb became to Christians a symbol of Christ, just as the time of the Jewish Passover became the time of the Christian Easter. But though the lamb was originally a purely religious representation, it has now become one of the other Easter symbols loved by children.

This book has been written to help you celebrate Easter in a way that will bring added joy to you and those you love. It is quite humbly offered as a guide and supplement to providing the creature comforts we have come to regard as pleasant customs, though they are entirely secondary to the great religious meaning of the season.

I

Lenten Dishes Come First

Lent is full of meatless days. Sometimes it is hard for the menu-planner to think up enough variety to prevent family meals from being boring under such circumstances. It oughtn't to be that hard, really! There's a wealth of other protein mainstays to fall back upon, and each can be cooked in a variety of ways. Here's the time to get working on your best sauces to give color, variety, and flavor to the fish, vegetable, egg, and cheese dishes you serve. Following are some suggestions which you can use for luncheons, suppers, and/or dinners. I think they will make your Lenten meals delectable, if that's what you'd like to accomplish. Just try them and see!

EGG AND CHEESE DISHES

Springtime Omelet

6 eggs
1 cup grated cheese
3 tablespoons minced parsley

1 medium-sized ripe tomato, chopped
Salt and pepper

Beat eggs lightly. Add other ingredients and mix well. Pour into lightly buttered skillet and cook over low heat, lifting sides occasionally to let liquid run under, until desired degree of doneness is reached. Fold and serve at once. Serves 4.

Cheese Soufflé

3 tablespoons butter
3 tablespoons flour
1 cup milk
½ cup grated Swiss cheese
½ cup grated Parmesan cheese

½ teaspoon salt
Few grains cayenne
4 egg yolks
4 egg whites
1 tablespoon minced chives

Melt butter; blend in flour smoothly. Add milk and stir until thickened. Add cheese and stir until entirely blended. Add salt and cayenne. Remove from heat. Beat egg yolks lightly and add to first mixture. Cool. Beat egg whites stiff and fold into cooled mixture. Fold in chives. Pour into ungreased baking dish large enough so that it is only two thirds full. Cook in 375 degree F. oven 25-30 minutes, or until puffed high and delicately brown. Serves 4.

Pot Cheese Dishes

Pot cheese or cottage cheese (the creamed variety) is low in calories, if that interests you, and has good protein value. It is particularly delicious served with finely-chopped fresh scallions, tomatoes, radishes, and cucumbers stirred into it, and a bowl of sour cream on the side. A fresh grind of pepper adds a lot, too.

A couple of canned peach or pear halves with pot cheese also make a fine dish for lunch or supper. The cheese always looks prettier if a mound of it is served in a lettuce leaf.

To tempt appetites and, perhaps, to make a more guestlike-appearing dish for Lenten luncheons or suppers, try one of these molded salads.

Jellied Peach-Cheese Ring

1 package cherry-flavored gelatin	1 box quick-frozen sliced peaches
Dash of salt	2 tablespoons peach juice
1 cup hot water	1½ cups cottage cheese, finely sieved
¾ cup cold water	

Dissolve gelatin and salt in hot water. Add cold water. Defrost and drain peaches. To drained peaches add peach juice, and let stand 15 minutes. Add 1 cup of the gelatin mixture. Chill until firm.

Chill remaining gelatin until slightly thickened. Place in a bowl of ice and water and whip with a rotary egg beater until fluffy and thick like whipped cream. Fold in cottage cheese, mixing well. Turn into 1½-quart ring mold. Chill until firm. Unmold onto salad greens. Spoon the chilled, jellied peaches into the center of this ring. Serves 6-8.

Creamy Cheese Mold

1 package lemon gelatin
1 cup hot water
½ cup cold water
1 ½ teaspoons vinegar
¾ teaspoon salt
3 tablespoons finely-chopped green pepper
2 tablespoons chopped

pimiento
½ cup mayonnaise
¼ teaspoon paprika
1 teaspoon minced onion
½ cup milk
½ cup cottage cheese
½ cup diced cucumber or celery

Dissolve gelatin in hot water. Add cold water, vinegar, and salt. Add 2 tablespoons cold water to ½ cup of mixture and pour into an 8' x 4' x 3-inch loaf pan or large mold. Chill until slightly thickened. Add 1 tablespoon of the green pepper and 1 of the pimiento. Chill until firm.

Combine mayonnaise, paprika, onion, milk, and remaining gelatin. Beat with a rotary egg beater to blend. Chill. When slightly thickened, place in a bowl of ice and water and whip with the rotary beater until fluffy and thick. Fold in remaining ingredients. Turn onto firm gelatin. Chill until firm. Unmold on crisp lettuce. Garnish with radish roses. Serves 4-6.

Eggs Poached with Mushrooms

2 teaspoons butter or margarine
4-ounce can sliced mushrooms
Dash powdered orégano
Salt and pepper

4 eggs
4 slices toast
Water cress

Melt fat in a large, heavy skillet. Add mushrooms with liquid. Heat gently. Sprinkle with orégano, salt, and pepper. Break eggs carefully into the frying pan, spacing them evenly. Cover tightly. Cook over low heat 3 to 5 minutes. Serve on hot toast, garnished with water cress. Serves 4.

Eggs Diabolo

4 tablespoons butter or margarine	Dash powdered basil
	Dash dry mustard
1 clove garlic	1 teaspoon minced parsley
1 small onion, minced	¼ teaspoon salt
1 cup tomato pulp	Pepper to taste
½ cup water	8 eggs
¼ teaspoon powdered thyme	Buttered toast points

Melt fat in a saucepan. Split garlic and stick a toothpick into each half. Sauté 2 to 3 minutes in the fat. Add minced onion, and cook over low heat about 10 minutes. Add tomato pulp and water and seasonings. Cook 10 minutes longer. Remove the garlic pieces. Pour sauce into an oblong baking dish. Into the sauce, break the eggs, spacing them evenly. Cover tightly. Bake in 350 degree F. oven until eggs are set (about 20 minutes). To serve, edge the dish with buttered toast points. Serves 4 or 8.

Deviled Eggs Mornay

6 hard-cooked eggs	2 tablespoons butter
2 tablespoons mayonnaise (about)	2 tablespoons flour
	1 cup light cream
¼ teaspoon dry mustard	½ cup grated Swiss cheese
3 large stuffed olives, chopped	2 egg yolks

Split eggs lengthwise and remove yolks. Mash with a fork. Mix with mayonnaise and chopped olives and stuff into whites. Place in shallow baking dish.

Melt butter. Carefully blend in flour until smooth. Add cream and stir until thickened. Add cheese and stir until absorbed. Beat egg yolks lightly and add a little of the sauce to them, beating constantly. Add yolks to sauce and beat in well. Pour sauce around eggs and bake in 400 degree F. oven until slightly brown and bubbling (about 20 minutes). Serves 4-6.

Smoky Scrambled Eggs
(For each person)

Butter or margarine

2 eggs

½ cup grated smoked Cheddar cheese

¼ teaspoon salt

Dash cayenne pepper

1 tablespoon minced parsley

Melt fat in a skillet. Beat eggs with a fork and beat in grated cheese. Pour into skillet and stir constantly over low heat until almost done to the consistency you like. Add seasonings and parsley, and stir constantly a minute more.

FISH AND SEA FOOD DISHES

Crab Cakes

4 tablespoons butter or
  margarine
1 medium-sized green pepper,
  chopped
1 medium-sized onion,
  chopped
½ teaspoon dry mustard
2 tablespoons Worcestershire
  sauce

1 teaspoon salt
Dash of pepper
½ cup flour
1 cup milk (scant)
1 pound crab meat (fresh or
  canned)
Cracker meal
1 egg, beaten

Melt butter or margarine. Sauté green pepper and onion until soft but not browned. Add mustard, Worcestershire, salt, and pepper. Blend in flour. Scald milk and add, stirring until thickened. Add crab meat. Mix well and chill thoroughly. Form into round cakes, one inch thick. Dip cakes into cracker meal, beaten egg, and then into cracker meal again. Fry in hot deep fat until nicely browned. Serve with sauce below. Serves 4.

Sauce for Crab Cakes

¼ cup butter
1½ teaspoons mustard
1 tablespoon chili powder
1 teaspoon sugar
1½ teaspoons salt

1 (8-ounce) can condensed
  tomato soup
½ can water
1 tablespoon vinegar

Melt butter. Blend in mustard, chili powder, sugar, and salt. Add soup, water, and vinegar, and mix well. Simmer gently until heated through.

Flaked Fish Casserole
(Plate 1)

2 egg yolks

2 cups milk

2 tablespoons quick-cooking tapioca

1 ½ teaspoons salt

Dash pepper

½ cup finely-cut celery

1 ½ teaspoons minced onion

2 cups flaked cooked fish

2 tablespoons chopped parsley

2 egg whites, stiffly beaten

½ cup bread crumbs, buttered

Mix egg yolks with a small amount of the milk in a saucepan. Add remaining milk, tapioca, salt, pepper, celery, and onion, and mix well. Place over medium heat and cook until mixture comes to a boil, stirring constantly. Remove from heat. Add fish and parsley. Add very gradually to beaten egg whites, folding in thoroughly. Turn into greased 2-quart baking dish. Cover with crumbs. Bake in 350 degree F. oven 50 minutes, or until browned. Serves 6.

Deviled Eggs with Shrimp on Rice

6 hard-cooked eggs

3 tablespoons mayonnaise

4 tablespoons vinegar

¼ teaspoon salt

⅛ teaspoon dry mustard

Dash of pepper

1 cup cooked or canned shrimp

1 ⅓ cups packaged, precooked

rice

1 ½ cups water

½ teaspoon salt

3 tablespoons butter

3 tablespoons flour

2 cups top milk or light cream

1 ½ teaspoons grated onion

1 teaspoon curry powder

Cut eggs in half. Remove yolks and force through a sieve. Add mayonnaise, vinegar, salt, mustard, and pepper, and mix well. Cut shrimp into small pieces and add. Fill egg whites with the mixture.

Combine rice, water, and salt in saucepan. Mix just until all rice is moistened. Bring quickly to a boil over high heat, uncovered, fluffing rice gently once or twice with a fork. (Do *not* stir.) Cover and remove from heat. Let stand 10 minutes.

Meanwhile, melt butter in saucepan. Add flour and stir until blended. Then add liquid gradually, stirring constantly. Add onion and curry powder. Cook and stir until sauce is smooth and thickened.

Place deviled eggs on bed of rice and top with the sauce. Serves 4.

PLATE 1 FLAKED FISH CASSEROLE

Fish Pudding

1 pound halibut	Dash of nutmeg
2 egg whites	½ teaspoon cornstarch
½ teaspoon salt	½ cup heavy cream
Dash of pepper	1½ cups milk

Remove all skin and bones from fish. Put through the finest blades of the grinder twice. Add one egg white, and grind again. Add all other ingredients except cream and milk, and grind again. Beat in electric mixer for 30 minutes, adding cream and milk gradually. Place in buttered baking dish and bake in 350 degree F. oven for 1 hour. The pudding will be solid and dry enough to slice. Serve with cream sauce—or, to be really elegant, with a lobster sauce. Serves 4.

Fish Fillets with Cheese Sauce

1 pound fish fillets	1 tablespoon flour
1 onion, sliced	1 cup milk
Dash thyme	¾ cup grated cheese
1 tablespoon butter	Salt and pepper

Poach fillets in water in a skillet to which a few slices of onion and a dash of thyme have been added, 8-10 minutes. Drain and place in shallow baking dish. Melt butter. Blend in flour smoothly. Add milk and stir until thickened. Add cheese and stir constantly until melted. Season to taste with salt and pepper. Pour over fillets and run under broiler flame until sauce bubbles and browns (about 5 minutes). Serves 4.

Fresh Salmon Hollandaise

4 salmon steaks
Salt and pepper
Butter or margarine

1 recipe Hollandaise Sauce
(page 41)

Season salmon steaks with salt and pepper. Sauté in butter or margarine, browning very lightly on both sides, until done through (about 15 minutes for inch-thick slices). Meantime, make Hollandaise Sauce and serve it in a separate bowl. Serves 4.

Creamed Tuna Fish with Herbed Rice

1⅓ cups packaged precooked rice
1½ cups water
½ teaspoon salt
Dash thyme, rosemary, basil, or savory
¼ cup sliced onions
2 tablespoons butter

1 (8-ounce) can cream of mushroom soup
½ cup milk
1 (7-ounce) can solid pack tuna
2 tablespoons chopped ripe olives
Dash of pepper

Combine rice, water, salt and herb in saucepan. Mix just enough to moisten all rice. Bring quickly to a boil over high heat, uncovered, fluffing rice gently once or twice with a fork. (Do *not* stir.) Cover and remove from heat. Let stand 10 minutes.

Meanwhile, sauté onions in butter until golden. Add soup and milk. Heat, stirring occasionally. Then add tuna, drained and flaked, olives, and pepper. Mix and heat thoroughly. May be served mixed with rice, poured over rice, or put into a casserole, topped with buttered crumbs, and browned under a flame. Serves 4.

Crab Meat Spanish Rice

¼ cup bacon drippings, butter, or margarine
1 medium-sized onion, thinly sliced (about ½ cup)
½ medium-sized green pepper, diced (about ⅓ cup)
1⅓ cups packaged precooked rice

1¾ cups hot water
2 (eight-ounce) cans tomato sauce
1 teaspoon salt
Dash of pepper
1 cup canned or cooked fresh crab meat

Melt fat in saucepan. Add onion, green pepper, and rice. Cook and stir over high heat until lightly browned. Add water, tomato sauce, salt, and pepper. Mix well. Bring quickly to a boil. Cover tightly and simmer 10 minutes. Add crab meat, mix, and heat thoroughly. Serves 4.

Crab Bisque
(Plate 2)

1½ tablespoons quick-cooking tapioca
1 teaspoon salt
Dash pepper
Dash paprika
1 teaspoon dry mustard

1 tablespoon minced onion
3 cups milk
1 cup (6½-ounce can) crab meat, drained and flaked
2 tablespoons butter
1 tablespoon chopped parsley

Combine tapioca, salt, pepper, paprika, dry mustard, onion, and milk in top of double boiler. Place over rapidly boiling water, and cook 10-12 minutes, stirring frequently. Add crab meat, butter, and parsley. Mix and keep over boiling water until thoroughly heated. Serve in cups or bowls. Serves 4.

Lox, Bagels, and Cream Cheese

"Lox" is smoked salmon. Bagels are very hard, doughnut-shaped rolls, smooth and light brown on the outside. The two combined with cream cheese make an absolutely delicious luncheon, supper, or as originally intended, breakfast! Split the bagels, toast them lightly, spread with cream cheese and lay a good slice of smoked salmon on top.

PLATE 2 CRAB BISQUE

MISCELLANEOUS LENTEN DISHES

Eggplant Caviar

1 large eggplant	½ cup olive oil
1 large onion	1 teaspoon salt
1 clove garlic	Fresh ground black pepper
2 large tomatoes	½ teaspoon sugar

Peel eggplant and cut into cubes. Boil in lightly salted water until soft (about 20 minutes). Drain well. Peel onion and garlic and place in chopping bowl with cut up tomatoes and the eggplant. Chop well. Add oil, salt, pepper, and sugar, and mix thoroughly. Chill well. Serve as a first course or a luncheon dish with dark pumpernickel and butter. Serves 4-6.

Meatless Minestrone

2 carrots	½ cup cranberry beans
2 stalks celery	2 sprigs parsley
1 cup green beans	3 cups boiling water
1 leek	2 small tomatoes
1 onion	½ cup chopped cabbage
2 small potatoes, pared	¼ pound spinach
1½ tablespoons olive oil	½ cup shell macaroni
1½ tablespoons butter	Salt and pepper
½ cup peas	Grated Parmesan cheese
½ cup lima beans	

Cut up carrots, celery, green beans, leek, onion, and potatoes. Heat oil and butter in a large kettle. Add cut vegetables, peas, lima and cranberry beans, and parsley. Stir over low heat for 10 minutes, or until vegetables make their own juice. Add water and tomatoes, cut up fine. Cook at a slow boil for 25 minutes. Add cabbage, spinach, and macaroni, and cook 20 minutes longer. Season to taste with salt and pepper. Serve with Parmesan cheese to sprinkle over top. As a main dish this serves 4.

Mushroom Lasagna

8 ounces lasagna	1 cup light cream
1 pound fresh mushrooms	Salt and pepper
2 tablespoons butter or margarine	½ pound mozzarella cheese
2 tablespoons flour	Grated Parmesan cheese

Boil lasagna twenty minutes, or until tender, stirring frequently so that it won't stick together. Meantime clean and slice mushrooms. Melt butter and sauté mushrooms in it five minutes. Add flour and blend well. Add cream and stir until sauce is thickened. Season to taste with salt and pepper. Slice mozzarella thinly. When lasagna is done, drain well. In a baking dish make layers of lasagna, mushroom sauce and mozzarella until used up. Cover with grated Parmesan and bake in 400 degree oven 20-25 minutes or until mozzarella is melted and Parmesan lightly browned. Serves 4.

Asparagus Milanese

1 bunch asparagus (or 1 pack-   Salt and pepper
  age, quick-frozen)   4 slices toast
4 eggs   ⅓ cup grated Parmesan cheese

Cook asparagus and drain. Fry the eggs and season with salt
and pepper. Divide asparagus into four portions and put, on
slices of toast, into fire-proof plates. Place a fried egg on each
portion, sprinkle all with Parmesan cheese and run under the
broiler flame to brown lightly. Serves 4.

Vitamin Salad

1 package lemon gelatin   ½ cup diced celery
1 cup hot water   1 teaspoon chopped onion
1 cup cold water   2 tablespoons chopped mixed
1 tablespoon vinegar   pickles
1 teaspoon salt   1 cup cottage cheese
1 cup coarsely-chopped raw   ¼ teaspoon grated onion
  spinach   Mayonnaise
½ cup shredded raw carrots

Dissolve gelatin in hot water. Add cold water, vinegar, and salt.
Chill until slightly thickened. Fold in spinach, carrots, celery,
chopped onion, and pickles. Turn into ring mold. Chill until
firm. Unmold on crisp lettuce. Fill center of ring with mixed
cottage cheese and grated onion. Serve with mayonnaise.
Serves 6.

Pizza Pie

4⅔ cups flour, sifted	Salt and pepper
2 tablespoons lard	½ teaspoon oregano
¼ teaspoon salt	½ pound mozzarella cheese
1 envelope yeast	20 flat anchovy fillets
1 cup warm water	Olive oil
1 (Number 2) can tomatoes, drained	

On a pastry board mix flour, lard, salt, yeast, and water, and work them well with your hands until smooth. Place in a large bowl, cover with a cloth, and let rise in a warm place about 2 hours until doubled in bulk. Place on a floured board and pound lightly. Divide into two pieces, and stretch each piece over the bottom of a greased 12-inch pie pan.

Place tomatoes in the two pans and season with salt, pepper, and oregano. Slice mozzarella thin and place slices over tomatoes. Lay anchovy fillets over tops of pies. Sprinkle all with olive oil and bake in 400 degree F. oven about 20 minutes, or until edges of crust are crisp. Depending on appetites, this can serve 2 or 6!

Stuffed Pancakes

The Cakes

6 egg yolks	6 egg whites
⅔ cup flour (scant)	½ teaspoon salt
1 cup (or more) thin cream	

Beat yolks well. Blend flour with cream. Add to egg yolks. Fold in beaten whites and salt. The mixture should be thin. Bake pancakes 4-5 inches in diameter.

The Filling

1 pound mushrooms	2 tablespoons flour
1 onion	½ cup sour cream
4 tablespoons butter	2 hard-cooked eggs, chopped
½ teaspoon salt	1 teaspoon parsley, minced
Pepper	6 tablespoons grated cheese

Chop mushrooms coarsely. Put into ungreased pan over low heat and stir constantly until the juice begins to draw. Chop onion fine, brown it delicately in butter, and add to mushrooms with salt and pepper. Cook about 10 minutes over low heat. Sprinkle flour lightly over and blend gently. Add sour cream, mix, and simmer 2 minutes. Add chopped eggs and parsley. Spread mixture over pancakes and roll them up. Arrange side by side in a shallow casserole. Sprinkle with grated cheese. Brown under broiler flame. Serves 6-8.

Zucchini with Cheese and Eggs

4 small zucchini	⅔ cup grated Parmesan
4 tablespoons cream	Salt and pepper
1 egg	Butter (optional)
4 tablespoons butter, melted	

Cut unpeeled zucchini into quarter-inch slices. Put into saucepan with very little water and cook slowly, stirring frequently until water has evaporated. Mix with cream, egg slightly beaten, butter, and about half the cheese. Season to taste with salt and pepper. Place in a casserole and top with the remaining cheese, which may be very lightly dotted with butter, if desired. Bake in 400 degree F. oven until top is lightly browned (20-25 minutes). Serves 4.

2

All About Ham

Ham is our traditional Easter meat, and how wonderful it tastes after the fasting days of Lent! For most of us, Easter dinner without ham would be a sort of halfway feast. Sometimes, I think, people sadly miss out on ham for Easter because "a ham is too much for a small family" or some such reason. There's some delectable ham cut to fit the size of every family, so familiarize yourself with what to buy and happily follow tradition at Easter time.

MUST IT BE COOKED?

Most hams carry some sort of identification of type and also instructions for cooking. However, too many designations have confused the public for a long time.

Fully-cooked Ham is precisely what it says it is. It is thoroughly and completely cooked and may be eaten as is or reheated if desired.

Ready-to-Eat Ham is, it may surprise you to learn, not really ready to eat at all, if you care about the finest flavor and texture. It is probably *safe* to eat, but if you want it to be really good, you should treat it just like an uncooked ham.

Cook-Before-Eating on a ham means that it must be completely cooked before it is safe or palatable to eat.

Tenderized and Tendered hams simply make you the victim of advertising slogans. They do not, as with the terms Fully-Cooked and Cook-Before-Eating, tell you in government terminology the degree of heat to which the ham has been brought by the packer.

Canned Hams are fully cooked and ready to eat straight from the can, or to be reheated.

HOW MUCH TO BUY

A whole ham looks like a lot of meat—and it is, but if you're a large family or are going to have a lot of guests or realize the variety of dishes you can make with what's left over—a full ham is the buy for you. Canned boned ham is a wonderful trouble-saver for large parties. If, however, you see no possibility of doing away with that much ham in the foreseeable future, half a ham, a ham slice, or a ham butt will make a good buy for you.

In buying half a ham, note whether the ham is cut exactly in half or whether one or more center slices have been taken off it, which will leave smaller-sized butt and shank ends. The shank end with the center cut left on is likely to cost more per pound because it is the choice portion with the least bone. A Picnic ham (smoked pork shoulder) might be just the right size for you, as it is definitely smaller than the full-sized ham. Picnics are fully cooked and may be heated if you wish. They also come fruited —very gay and festive looking and ready to serve cold.

HOW LONG WILL HAM KEEP?

This is a point, of course, which may help you make up your mind which cut to buy. Hams must be kept in the refrigerator. They do not freeze well. They should be eaten within a week's time. You can, however, freeze canned ham, unopened, and it will keep very well.

BAKED HAM

A whole baked ham is certainly the most traditional of all Easter ham dishes. A beautiful glaze and pretty decorations make it the most gala entrée possible. Treat a half-ham just as you would a whole one.

If your ham or Picnic has an artificial casing, remove that before cooking. Either slit the casing lengthwise and strip it off or cut off both ends of the casing and unwind it spiral-wise.

Heat oven to 325 degrees F. Place either a Fully-cooked or Cook-Before-Eating ham, fat-side up, on a rack in an open roasting pan with no water added. Use the cooking schedules below for whichever variety you're cooking (or bring the Cook-

Before-Eating one to 150 degrees, and the Fully-Cooked to 130 degrees on your meat thermometer). Remove from the oven and turn heat up to 450 degrees. Pour off the drippings. Remove skin. Score fat. Glaze the ham (as suggested page 35) and return to the oven to brown (about 15 minutes).

During baking, if you like, you may baste the ham with pine-apple juice, cider, Madeira, dry red or white wine, or (for great elegance!) with champagne.

Cooking Time for Cook-Before-Eating Ham

Weight	Time
5-8 pounds	2 ¾ hours
8-10 pounds	2 ¾ —3 hours
10-12 pounds	3 —3 ½ hours
12-15 pounds	3 ½ —4 hours
15-18 pounds	4 —4 ½ hours
18-22 pounds	4 ½ —5 ½ hours
22-24 pounds	5 ½ —6 hours

If you prefer, you can *boil* the Cook-Before-Eating ham and then glaze it. Use the same cooking time as that given above for baking.

Heating Time for Fully-cooked Ham

Weight	Time
8-10 pounds	2 hours
10-12 pounds	2 —2 ½ hours
12-15 pounds	2 ½ —3 hours
15-18 pounds	3 —3 ⅓ hours
18-22 pounds	3 ½ —4 ¼ hours

GLAZES FOR BAKED HAM

Brown Sugar: Pat a good layer of sugar gently onto the fat. Decorate with whole cloves.

Honey: Spread honey over fat with a pastry brush. Cloves here, too, if you like.

Orange Marmalade: Spread over fat with a spatula.

Apricot Jam: Spread over fat with a spatula.

Hot-sweet Glaze: Spread Bahamian mustard thinly over fat. Then pat on a good layer of brown sugar.

GARNISHES FOR BAKED HAM

Easter Egg: Shell hard-cooked eggs. Put a few drops of green vegetable coloring into one small bowl of water and a few drops of yellow into another. Dip half the eggs into each to tint them delicately. If you like, trim off white at one end, so that part of the yolk shows. Surround ham with eggs in alternate colors, separated by sprigs of parsley.

Flowers: Decorate the ham platter with Easter blossoms in various spring colors. Be sure to have a plate handy so that the flowers may be removed to it after the total effect has been admired, as the carver's convenience must be considered.

Vegetables: Make "flowers" out of radishes, turnips, and carrot curls to lend gaiety to the platter. These may be served with the ham.

Ham Gravy

When you remove the ham from its long slow baking, put it on a platter, pour off the clear drippings and save for future use. Pour the brown drippings into a skillet and return the ham to the pan for finishing. Make gravy in the skillet, using the proportion of 3 tablespoons drippings to 3 tablespoons flour, stirred until smooth, and 2 cups of milk or water added. Stir constantly until thickened. If you have not used wine in basting, the addition of sherry to taste in this gravy is delicious.

Sauce for Ham

Heat ½ pint cream, 2 tablespoons dry mustard, and ⅓ cup sugar in a double boiler, mixing thoroughly. Beat 2 egg yolks and add 1 tablespoonful of the hot sauce to them, mixing well. Add this to the sauce and beat with a wire whisk until thickened. Beat in ⅓ cup vinegar. The sauce is in the end quite thin.

Ham Butts

These little hams are best boiled or simmered first (about 45 minutes per pound). They may then be baked like big hams, if you like.

HAM SLICES

This term means many things to many people. You can buy a slice 2 inches thick. In this case, you will cook it in a 350 degree F. oven, basted as you like, for about 2 hours. However, if you prefer a slice about an inch thick, or even a little less, you can pan-fry it with great effect, using a little extra fat to make it brown quickly, if necessary, then pour in water, milk, pineapple juice, or what you will; cover and simmer over very low heat until tender and well-flavored (about 20 to 30 minutes). Here are some of my favorite ham-slice recipes.

Ham Slice with Marsala Sauce

1 slice fully-cooked ham, 1 inch thick	1 tablespoon cornstarch
2 tablespoons butter	¾ cup Marsala (or sherry) wine

Brown ham rapidly on both sides in skillet. Remove from skillet; add butter. When butter is melted, stir in cornstarch smoothly. Add wine and stir until smooth and slightly thickened. Add ham, cover, and simmer over very low heat about 15 minutes. Serves 2-3.

Ham Baked in Milk

1 slice ham, 1 inch thick	Brown sugar
Prepared mustard	Milk to cover

Place ham in shallow baking dish. Spread top thinly with prepared mustard and sprinkle with brown sugar. Pour in milk to *almost* cover the ham. Bake in 350 degree F. oven for 1 hour. Serves 2-3.

Pineapple Ham Slice

1 slice fully-cooked ham, 1 inch thick

1 (9-ounce) can crushed pine-apple

Pan-fry ham rapidly to brown, adding a little fat if necessary. When brown on both sides, pour in juice from pineapple, cover pan, and simmer about 20 minutes. Add crushed pineapple and leave on stove just long enough to heat fruit thoroughly. Serves 2-3.

Ham Slice with Apricots

1 slice fully-cooked ham, 1 inch thick

⅓ cup water

Apricot jam

Place ham in baking dish with water and cook in 350 degree F. oven long enough to heat through (about 20 minutes). Spread with jam, and run under broiler flame until jam is bubbling and beginning to brown a little. Serves 2-3.

Ham with Red Gravy

This requires country-cured Smithfield Ham, which is usually obtainable in the South or in sections of large cities in other parts of the country where southerners shop a lot. The ham is very salty and so should be soaked at least 6 hours before cooking.

2 slices country-cured Smithfield Ham, ½ inch thick

¾ cup boiling water

Remove hard black rind from ham slices, after soaking. Brown in ungreased heavy skillet at fairly high heat, but do not burn. Fry each side 5-7 minutes. Remove slices to a platter, pour off all but about 1½ tablespoons fat and place pan on heat so that it becomes smoking hot. Add water, allow to boil up and be sure to scrape all the "fry" into the gravy. Pour over ham slices and serve with hominy grits. The gravy is not always red in color, but it always tastes wonderful!

LEFTOVER HAM DISHES

Ham and Macaroni

8 ounces elbow macaroni	½ cup cream
½ cup butter	Salt and pepper
½ cup flour	1 cup minced cooked ham
1½ cups milk	Grated Parmesan cheese

Cook macaroni in boiling salted water 10 to 15 minutes and drain. Melt butter, add flour, and stir over low heat to blend smoothly. Add milk and cream and cook until thickened, stirring constantly. Season to taste with salt and pepper. Add cooked macaroni and ham. Mix well. Put into a baking dish, sprinkle with grated Parmesan cheese, and bake in 400 degree F. oven until nicely browned (20-25 minutes). Serves 4-6.

Ham Croquettes

4 tablespoons butter or   1 tablespoon minced onion
  margarine   1 egg yolk
4 tablespoons flour   2 cups minced ham
1 cup rich milk or cream   Bread crumbs
¼ teaspoon salt   1 whole egg
Good grind fresh pepper

Melt fat. Blend in flour smoothly. Add milk or cream and cook, stirring constantly, until thickened. Add seasonings, onion, and egg yolk, beating well to blend. Add ham. Chill mixture. Shape croquettes as desired. Roll in fine bread crumbs, then in beaten egg, then in crumbs. Fry, a few at a time, in deep fat until golden brown. Drain on absorbent paper. Makes 10-12 croquettes. Good served with the following sauce:

Roz's 1-2-3-4 Sauce

1 teaspoon French's mustard   4 tablespoons sour cream
2 tablespoons cold water   Dash garlic powder
3 tablespoons Escoffier Sauce   Pinch orégano
  Diable

Mix all together. Let stand 30 minutes before serving. It should not be chilled.

Ham en Brochette
(For each person)

4 one-inch squares cooked ham   3 small mushrooms
3 one-inch squares Cheddar   3 pineapple chunks
  cheese

On big single-portion skewers alternate the above ingredients according to your fancy. Cook about 5 inches from hot broiler flame, turning as they brown, until brown on all sides (about 8 minutes).

Eggs Benedict
(For each person)

1 English muffin   2-3 tablespoons Hollandaise
2 thin slices cooked ham   Sauce
2 eggs

Toast muffin halves. Warm ham in skillet, but do not brown. Poach eggs.

Put ham slices on muffin halves, poached eggs on ham, and top with Hollandaise Sauce (see below). Wonderful party breakfast, luncheon, or supper dish, but don't try to make it for more than four. As you will observe, everything has to be done at once!

Hollandaise Sauce

½ cup butter   Dash of salt
2 egg yolks   Few grains of cayenne
1 tablespoon lemon juice

Melt butter. Mix egg yolks with lemon juice in top of double boiler, over hot, *not boiling*, water. Add butter gradually, beating constantly (preferably with a wire whisk but a fork will do), until sauce thickens to the consistency you like. Remove from heat at once and add seasonings. If the sauce should crack, simply beat in a little boiling water and it will come back to a smooth consistency.

Casserole of Ham and Sauerkraut

2 cups cubed cooked ham

1 can sauerkraut

1 teaspoon caraway seeds

1 pint sour cream

Dash of cayenne

Mix all ingredients together and place in casserole. Bake in 400 degree F. oven 20-25 minutes. Serves 4-6.

Ham Loaf

2 cups ground fresh pork

2 cups ground cooked ham

1 cup cracker meal

1 cup milk

2 eggs, well beaten

6 tablespoons catsup

6 tablespoons brown sugar

6 tablespoons catsup

Have the butcher grind the pork. Mix it well with the ham. Add cracker meal, milk, eggs, and the first 6 tablespoons of catsup. Mix well. Form into a loaf or pack lightly into a loaf pan and bake in 375 degree F. oven half an hour. Mix brown sugar with second 6 tablespoons catsup, and spread over loaf. Continue baking for another half hour. Serves 6.

HOW TO CARVE A HAM

PLATE 3 STEP 1   *PLATE 4* STEP 2

HOW TO CARVE HAM

(Plates 3-6)

Place ham platter so that fullest side of ham is away from the carver. First cut a few slices from the side opposite the full side. This provides a firm base for carving. Turn the ham onto the cut section, plunge fork into the butt end, and hold fork firmly during the carving.

Start at the shank end and make a long, curving horizontal cut, following the length of the leg bone until the bone in the butt end is reached (Plate 3). This enables the carver to lift out slices as they are carved with no trouble at all.

Next remove a wedge-shaped cut to permit the cutting of deep, uniform slices (Plate 4).

Now, start slicing at the wedge-shaped cut, using firm, long slicing strokes slanting down to the leg bone (Plate 5).

Remove slices for easy serving to side of platter (Plate 6). The ham may now be turned back to its original position on the platter and slices cut at right angles to the bone. These slices are not so large as those from the cushion side, but are just as good eating.

HOW TO CARVE A HAM

PLATE 5 STEP 3   *PLATE 6* STEP 4

3

Easter Cakes and Breads

Gay, pretty, and delectable cakes are an integral part of the joyous Easter season, so are unusual breads. The Russian Orthodox people, in particular, have always made their Easter cake a must at their wonderful Easter parties. Here's a recipe for it which I have worked out over the years from those of Russian friends. It's infallible, easy to make, and utterly delicious. Do try it!

EASTER CAKES

Paskha

(Russian Easter cake)

2½ pounds cottage cheese
1 cup sugar
¼ pound almonds, blanched and chopped
¾ cup mixed candied fruits
1 teaspoon vanilla
½ teaspoon salt

½ pound sweet butter
½ pint heavy cream
1 whole egg
2 egg yolks
Fresh flowers, and jelly eggs for garnish

Force cottage cheese through a sieve. Blend with sugar, almonds, fruits, vanilla, and salt. Melt butter. Add cream, whole egg, and egg yolks. Stir constantly over low heat until thickened. Remove from heat and cool. Mix with cottage cheese mixture and beat well.

Line a 5½-inch flower pot (or two 3-inch ones) with a linen napkin and pour the mixture in. Fold napkin lightly over and place a weight on top. Place in a pan to catch the small amount of moisture which will seep through the hole in the bottom and put into the refrigerator for at least 12 hours. When ready to serve, lift gently from pot with napkin, place on a serving dish, and remove napkin carefully. Decorate with fresh flowers and little jelly eggs, pressed into the side of the cake to form a cross. Serve in slices. Serves 12-15. Will keep a week if well refrigerated.

Lamb Cake

(Plate 7)

2 ¼ cups cake flour	¾-1 cup milk
2 ¼ teaspoons double-acting baking powder	1 teaspoon vanilla
¼ teaspoon salt	Seven-Minute Frosting
½ cup shortening	Green coloring
1 cup sugar	1 ½ cups shredded coconut
2 eggs, unbeaten	Raisins
	1 maraschino cherry

Sift flour once, measure, add baking powder and salt, and sift again.

Cream shortening, add sugar gradually, and cream together until light and fluffy. Add eggs, one at a time, beating thoroughly after each. Add flour, alternately with milk, a small amount at a time, beating after each addition until smooth. (Use a little less milk with butter, margarine, or lard than with vegetable shortening.) Add vanilla.

Pour batter into face-half of well-greased lamb mold. Round batter slightly in regions of head and neck. Cover with back of mold and wire mold together. Place mold face-down on baking sheet and bake in hot oven (450 degrees F.) 15 minutes. Reduce heat to 350 degrees and bake 45 minutes longer.

Take mold from oven and open, removing back of mold. Allow cake to cool in face of mold about 5 minutes. Then loosen from sides of mold and remove carefully. Stand lamb cake on cake rack until cool.

Meanwhile, make recipe again, and pour batter into a 13 x 9 x 2-inch pan. Bake in moderate oven (375 degrees) 35 minutes, or until done. Cool cake in pan on cake rack for 5 minutes, then loosen from sides with spatula, turn out, and turn right-side up on rack to cool.

Frost oblong cake with Seven-Minute Frosting. Tint ½ cup coconut a delicate green and sprinkle on top to represent grass. Then frost lamb cake with remaining Seven-Minute Frosting, and cover with untinted coconut. Use raisins for eyes and nose and a slice of maraschino cherry for mouth. Place lamb on center of cake base.

PLATE 7 LAMB CAKE

Easter Pineapple Cake

(Plate 8)

2 cups *sifted* cake flour	½ teaspoon vanilla
1 ⅓ cups sugar	½ teaspoon lemon extract
2 teaspoons double-action baking powder	1 cup milk
1 teaspoon salt	1 unbeaten egg and 2 un- beaten egg yolks (⅓-½
⅓ cup vegetable shortening	cup)

Grease two round 8-inch layer cake pans generously and dust with flour.

Sift dry ingredients into a bowl. Add shortening, flavorings, and ⅔ of the milk. Beat 2 minutes at medium speed with the electric mixer or 300 vigorous strokes by hand. Scrape sides and bottom of bowl constantly. Add remaining milk and eggs. Beat 2 minutes more, scraping bowl constantly. Pour into prepared pans. Bake 25 to 30 minutes at 375 degrees F. Cool. Spread Pineapple Filling between layers, reserving about ½ cup for the top. Frost sides and outer edge of top (1 ½ inches wide) with Fluffy White Frosting. Spread remainder of filling in center onto top of cake.

Pineapple Filling

½ cup sugar	¾ to 1 cup crushed pineapple, drained
Dash salt	
3 tablespoons cornstarch	1 tablespoon butter
¾ cup pineapple juice	1 teaspoon lemon juice

Mix sugar, salt, and cornstarch in saucepan. Slowly stir in pineapple juice, then the crushed pineapple. Cook over low heat,

PLATE 8   EASTER PINEAPPLE CAKE

stirring constantly, until mixture thickens and boils. Boil 1
minute. Remove from heat. Stir in butter and lemon juice. Cool
thoroughly before placing on cake.

Fluffy White Frosting

½ cup water   2 egg whites
½ cup sugar   1 teaspoon vanilla

Bring sugar and water to the boil and continue boiling until mixture spins a thin thread when dropped from the end of a spoon.
Beat egg whites very stiff and add sugar-water sirup to them, a
tablespoonful at a time, beating thoroughly with each addition.
(The electric mixer is wonderful for this.) Add vanilla, and continue beating until frosting is the consistency you like. If it
hardens before spreading, beat in a few drops of hot water. This
makes enough for top and sides of two layers.

Easter Bunny and Chick Cupcakes

(Plate 9)

2½ cups sifted cake flour
3 tablespoons double-acting
  baking powder
1 teaspoon salt
1½ cups sugar
½ cup shortening
1 cup milk
1 teaspoon vanilla

2 eggs, unbeaten
Fluffy White Frosting
Yellow coloring (optional)
Shredded coconut
Marshmallows
Cloves
Yellow string gumdrops

Measure flour, baking powder, salt, and sugar into sifter. Stir shortening just to soften. Sift in dry ingredients. Add ¾ cup of the milk and the vanilla. Mix until all flour is dampened. Then beat 2 minutes with the mixer or 300 strokes by hand. Add eggs and remaining milk (scant it a little if your shortening is butter, margarine, or lard), and beat 1 minute longer, or 150 strokes. Scrape the bowl often and well.

Spoon the batter into paper baking cups set in muffin tins, filling only half full. Bake in 375 degree F. oven 15 to 20 minutes, or until done. Cool.

Spread with Fluffy White Frosting (or tint half of it yellow for the chicks and use the rest for the bunnies). Sprinkle with shredded coconut. Make *chicks* by using a marshmallow for each head and whole cloves for the eyes. Use yellow string gumdrops, clipped, for the webbed feet and tails, and small pieces of gumdrop for the beaks. Attach with toothpicks.

To make *bunnies*, invert the cupcakes, frost with fluffy white frosting, sprinkle with shredded coconut. Use a whole marshmallow for each head, a half marshmallow for each tail, and small pieces for the ears. Insert whole cloves for the eyes and coconut strands for the whiskers. The recipe makes 24 cakes.

PLATE 9 EASTER BUNNY AND CHICK CUPCAKES

PLATE 10 EASTER SURPRISE CAKE

Easter Surprise Cake

(Plate 10)

1 baked 10-inch angel food
cake
1 package strawberry gelatin
1 cup hot water
1 cup cold water
½ cup heavy cream, whipped

1 cup heavy cream
3 tablespoons sugar
Dash salt
¼ teaspoon vanilla
Rosebud mints (optional)

Cut a ¾-inch horizontal slice from the top of the cake. Carefully remove center of cake, leaving a ½-inch shell. Place on a serving plate.

Dissolve gelatin in hot water. Add cold water. Chill until slightly thickened. Place in bowl of ice and water and whip with a rotary egg beater until fluffy and thick like whipped cream. Fold in the whipped cream. Turn into cake shell and cover with the top slice of cake. Wrap in waxed paper and chill 6-8 hours or overnight.

Before serving cake, combine cream, sugar, salt, and vanilla. Whip until light and fluffy. Spread over top and sides of cake and decorate with rosebud mints, if desired. Serve at once.

And don't waste the cake you removed from the center! Toast strips of it under the broiler. Or roll cubes of cake in tinted Seven-Minute Frosting and shredded coconut. Or douse bits of cake with a sprinkling of sherry and serve with custard sauce.

Yellow Daffodil Cake

(On frontispiece)

Preparations: Have shortening at room temperature. Line bottoms of pans with paper. Use two round 8- or 9-inch layer pans. Start oven for 350 degree F. heat. Sift flour once before measuring.

2 ¼ cups sifted cake flour	1 ½ teaspoons vanilla
½ cup shortening	¼ teaspoon almond extract
3 ¼ teaspoons double acting baking powder	4 egg whites, unbeaten
	Yellow coloring
1 teaspoon salt	Fluffy White Frosting
1 ½ cups sugar	Shredded coconut
1 cup milk	Daffodils for garnish

Stir shortening just to soften. Sift in dry ingredients. Add ¾ cup of the milk and the flavorings. Mix until all flour is dampened. Beat 2 minutes with electric mixer or 300 strokes by hand. Add egg whites and remaining milk, then beat 1 minute longer, or 150 strokes. To one-third of the batter, add a few drops of yellow coloring.

Put large spoonfuls of batter into pans, alternating colors. With a knife, cut carefully through the batter once in a wide zigzag course, to marble the cake. Bake in 350 degree F. oven 25-30 minutes. Cool.

Spread your favorite fluffy white frosting between layers and over top and sides of cake. Sprinkle generously with shredded coconut. Garnish cake with a few fresh daffodils at the base and one or two on top.

Easy Bunny Cake

2 "boughten" round cake layers   Spring flowers for garnish
Fluffy White Frosting

Lay one layer just as is, flat, on a large plate or platter. From the
second layer, cut a smaller round for the head and lay it in position above the body. Make round tail and tall ears out of cut-off
bits of cake. Cover generously with Fluffy White Frosting, and
serve surrounded by fresh spring flowers.

Easter Bonnet Place-Card Cookies
(Plate 11)

Here's a "fun" place card for an Easter party. Put the bonnets
into hat boxes, if you like—or just attach names to the cookies
themselves.

2 cups sifted cake flour	1 egg, unbeaten
1½ teaspoons double-acting baking powder	3 squares unsweetened choco-late, melted
½ teaspoon soda	2 tablespoons milk
¼ teaspoon salt	Marshmallows
½ teaspoon cinnamon	Thin White Icing
½ cup butter or other shortening	Green coloring
1 cup sugar	Shredded Coconut

After sifting flour once, measure, add baking powder, soda, salt,
and cinnamon. Sift 3 times. Cream shortening, add sugar gradu-

PLATE 11 EASTER BONNET PLACE-CARD COOKIES

ally, creaming until light and fluffy. Add egg and chocolate. Beat well. Add flour mixture, a small amount at a time, mixing well after each addition. Add milk. Chill thoroughly. Roll ⅛ inch thick on lightly floured board. Cut with floured 3-inch round or scalloped cooky cutter. Bake on ungreased baking sheet in 350 degree F. oven 9 minutes. Cut marshmallows in half crosswise and place slightly off center on warm cooky, or fasten in place on cooled cooky with a small amount of icing. The marshmallow forms the crown of the bonnet, the cooky the brim. Spread green-tinted Thin White Icing over the crown and around the edge of the brim. Sprinkle icing with shredded coconut. Decorate, if desired, with small cake decorations (like birds and rosettes) fastened in place with icing.

Thin White Icing

Blend ¾ cup confectioners' sugar with about 2 tablespoons milk.

Half-Egg Cake

This cake isn't made from half an egg—it just *looks* like one!

Pint box strawberries
1 pint heavy cream
Sugar to taste

2 "boughten" round cake layers
Sweetheart roses for garnish

Hull berries, mash, and drain them well. Whip cream and sweeten to taste. Stir in berries. Cut one cake layer in half and stand halves on cut-side with a bit of the strawberry cream between to hold them together. Cut a strip from the middle of the second layer so that you have two halves, smaller than the first two. Put these, on their cut-sides, next to the larger halves, again using strawberry cream to hold them together. Cover all generously with strawberry cream. This gives the effect of a half-egg. Put some tiny sweetheart roses into the top for decoration.

EASTER BREADS

Russian Kulich
(Easter bread—Plate 12)

1 cake compressed, or
  1 package dry yeast
¼ cup warm water
1 cup lukewarm milk
½ cup sugar
½ teaspoon salt
2 eggs, beaten
¼ cup raisins

¼ cup chopped blanched
  almonds
½ teaspoon vanilla
⅓ cup soft butter or other
  shortening
5–5¼ cups *sifted* flour

Colored candies (optional)

PLATE 12 RUSSIAN KULICH

Dissolve yeast in warm water. Stir in all ingredients except flour. Mix in flour until dough is possible to handle. Turn onto lightly-floured board. Knead until smooth and elastic. Round up in greased bowl; bring greased side up. Cover with damp cloth and let rise until hole remains when finger is pressed deeply into dough (double in bulk)—about 2 hours. Punch down; round up; let rise again until not quite double in bulk (about 30 minutes). Punch down; round up on board; cover and let rest 15 minutes.

Divide dough into halves. Cover one part with a damp cloth. Divide the other part into halves. Round up into two round bun-like shapes and place in well greased 1-pound shortening cans or two Number 2 cans, patting top of dough even. Dough will fill cans half full. Make rest of dough into rolls of any desired shapes, such as cloverleaf, etc. Cover, let rise until impression remains when dough is touched gently—about 1 hour.

Heat oven to 375 degrees F. Place cans on cooky sheet and bake 30-40 minutes. Lay a piece of brown paper over cans last half of baking time. As loaf bakes, it rises above top of can in mushroom or mosque-like shape, characteristic of old Russia's Easter bread. Remove from cans and cool on rack.

Bake rolls on lightly-greased cooky sheet about 10 minutes in 400 degree oven. Frost tops of loaves and brush rolls with small amount of Thin White Lemon Icing. Icing may be sprinkled with colored candies.

Thin White Lemon Icing

¾ cup sifted confectioner's   1 tablespoon warm milk
    sugar   (about)
 1 teaspoon lemon juice
Blend all ingredients smoothly.

PLATE 13   BUNNY FACES

Bunny Faces
(Plate 13)

1 cake compressed, or	1 teaspoon salt
1 package dry yeast	1 egg
¼ cup warm water	¼ cup soft shortening
¾ cup lukewarm milk	3½–3¾ cups sifted flour
¼ cup sugar	Thin White Icing

Dissolve yeast in warm water. Stir in all ingredients except flour. Mix in flour until dough is easy to handle. Turn onto lightly floured board; knead until smooth and elastic. Round up in greased bowl; bring greased side up. Cover with damp cloth, let rise until hole remains when finger is pressed deeply into dough (double in bulk)—about 2 hours. Punch down; round up; let rise again until not quite double—about 45 minutes. Punch down; round up on board. Cover and let rest 15 minutes.

Divide dough into 9 pieces. Shape each piece into a strip of dough 13 inches long. Tie each in a knot and place on a greased cooky sheet, pulling the ends of the knot up on the sheet to form the ears of a bunny. Let rise until impression remains when dough is touched gently—30-40 minutes.

Heat oven to 375 degrees F. Bake bunnies about 20 minutes. While still warm, ice and decorate with Thin White Icing. Make eyes and mouths of raisins and cinnamon candies.

Thin White Icing

Blend ¾ cup confectioners' sugar with about 2 tablespoons milk. Use part of icing to frost bunnies. Into remaining icing, blend additional confectioners' sugar so that icing is thick enough to hold its shape. Tint pink with food coloring. Use for whiskers, nose, eyebrows, and to outline ears.

PLATE 14

BUNNY BISCUITS

Bunny Biscuits
(Plate 14)

2 cups sifted flour	¾ teaspoon salt
2½ teaspoons double-action baking powder	5 tablespoons shortening
	¾ cup milk (about)

Sift flour once, measure, add baking powder and salt, and sift again. Cut in shortening. Add milk and stir with fork until soft dough is formed (about 20 strokes). Turn out onto lightly-floured board and knead 20 turns. Roll or pat ¼ inch thick. Cut twenty 1½-inch circles for bodies, twenty 1-inch circles for heads, forty 1 x ¼-inch strips for ears, and make twenty very small balls of dough for tails. Place large circles on ungreased baking sheet. Attach heads and ears by dampening edge of biscuits and pressing together. Attach small balls in same manner, placing one on top of each large circle to simulate a tail. Bake in hot oven (425 degrees F.) 10 minutes, or until done. Makes 20 bunnies.

Hot Cross Buns

 1 yeast cake
¼ cup lukewarm water
 1 cup milk
½ cup sugar
½ cup shortening
 1 egg, beaten

¼ cup shredded citron
¼ cup seedless raisins
 3 cups flour
½ teaspoon salt
Powdered sugar or Thin
     White Icing

Soften the yeast in the lukewarm water. Scald milk, add sugar
and shortening, and cool. Add the beaten egg, the yeast, citron,
raisins, and the flour, sifted with the salt. Knead and let rise to
double its bulk. Shape into buns, place on greased baking sheet,
and let rise until light. Brush with a little milk, and bake at 375
degrees F. for about 20 minutes. When done, cover with powdered sugar in the shape of a cross or do the same with a Thin
White Icing.

4

Easter Breakfasts and Luncheons

One of the pleasantest times to have a party any time of year is breakfast, whether it's for a group of guests or just for the family. At this joyous Easter time, the children are eager to begin celebrating at once, and even in entirely adult households, the whole spirit of fresh, new, wonderful things to eat pervades every meal of the day, perhaps most of all the first one. Here are menu suggestions. The starred recipes follow each menu.

M E N U   I

Strawberries on Their Stems *
Shad Roe and Bacon *
Creamed Potatoes
Corn Bread *
Marmalade
Coffee

Strawberries on Their Stems

If the berries are very sandy, wash them, but if not, don't. They're so much better if they needn't be washed. Do not hull them. Serve on individual plates with a little mound of powdered sugar in the center to dip them into.

Shad Roe

Shad roe can be so wonderful—and so unattractive—that it's worth the small amount of attention it takes to make this Easter treat come out perfectly. Here's how!

Wipe the roe gently with a damp cloth. Season it with salt and pepper and dredge lightly with flour. Fry in butter over medium heat so that roe is crusty on the outside, done through, but soft on the inside. It should not take more than 10 minutes to cook. If it begins popping (and breaking open), your heat is too high. If, by sad chance, you find the roe has dried out on the inside, split it and put a pat of butter in each side of each roe. Serve with crisp bacon. Depending upon size, serve a half or whole roe per person.

Corn Bread

1 cup yellow corn meal	1 egg, well beaten
¼ cup sugar	1 cup milk
½ teaspoon salt	¼ cup melted butter or
1 cup flour	margarine
4 teaspoons baking powder	

Mix and sift dry ingredients. Combine egg, milk, and shortening. Add to dry ingredients slowly, beating until smooth. Pour into buttered square pan and bake in 375 degree F. oven 20-25 minutes.

MENU II

Stewed Rhubarb
Double-Boiler Scrambled Eggs * with Chicken Livers Sauté *
Poppyseed French Bread *
Hot Mocha Drink *

Double-Boiler Scrambled Eggs

2 tablespoons butter or	½ cup sour cream
margarine	½ teaspoon salt
6 eggs	Fresh ground pepper

Melt butter in top of double boiler. Beat eggs with cream and seasoning and pour into double boiler, over hot, not boiling, water. A glass double boiler is ideal for this, as you can see what's going on. In any event, stir the eggs occasionally with a fork and serve them when they're soft (not runny, and not dried out). Serves 4.

Chicken Livers Sauté

½ pound chicken livers
Salt and pepper

Flour
Butter or margarine

Season livers with salt and pepper and dredge lightly with flour. Sauté in melted butter or margarine over medium heat until nicely brown on both sides. Do not dry out by overcooking; about 8 minutes is long enough. Serves 4, with eggs.

Poppyseed French Bread

4 tablespoons butter
1 tablespoon poppyseeds

1 loaf Brown 'n' Serve French bread

Soften butter at room temperature. Mix well with poppyseeds. Cut bread into 1-inch slices, down to, but not through, the bottom crust. Spread between slices with poppyseed butter. Place on shallow pan and bake according to instructions on package. It may take a little longer than instructions read, due to the butter, but in any case, be sure to get it done to a fine golden brown.

Hot Mocha Drink
(For each person)

2 heaping teaspoons instant sweet cocoa mix

1 heaping teaspoon instant coffee
Hot milk

Combine cocoa mix and instant coffee in serving cup. Add hot milk gradually, stirring to blend.

Baby Watermelon Quarters
Smoked Fish in Cream *   Peas
Coffee

Baby Watermelon

I just hope that those wonderful little watermelons which came on the market only recently will be available to everyone in the United States in no time flat. If you can't get them, serve pink grapefruit in their place and keep a bright eye out for these little beauties to arrive in your market. A quarter of one makes just about a perfect serving.

Smoked Fish in Cream

¾ pound smoked sturgeon
2 tablespoons butter or
   margarine
2 tablespoons flour

1 cup heavy cream
½ teaspoon salt
Fresh ground pepper
Paprika

Cut fish into bite-sized pieces (unless you buy it in a jar, already cut). Melt butter, blend in flour smoothly. Add cream, and stir until thickened. Season with salt and pepper. Add fish and hold over low heat until fish has heated through. Serve on slices of toast or bread fried in butter with a dash of paprika on top. Serves 4.

MENU IV

Iced Clam and Tomato Juice
Fruit Omelet *
Bunny Faces (page 59)
Coffee

Fruit Omelet

4 egg yolks
½ teaspoon salt
Pepper
4 tablespoons hot water
4 egg whites

2 tablespoons butter or
 margarine
1 cup well-drained fresh,
 canned, or quick-frozen fruit

Beat egg yolks with salt, pepper, and hot water until thick and lemon colored. Beat whites stiff and fold them into the yolk mixture. Butter a skillet or omelet pan well and pour in the mixture. Cook over low heat, turning the pan now and then so that the omelet will brown evenly. When it has puffed nicely and is delicately brown on the bottom transfer the pan to a 350 degree F. oven. The omelet is done when it can be touched lightly with the finger and not stick and is also firm. Remove from oven and fold.

Meantime, warm the fruit in top of a double boiler. You may use mixed fruits or just one fruit. Strawberries, thinly sliced, are particularly good. Whatever fruit you use must be drained thoroughly, or the liquid will spoil the omelet.

Pour the warm fruit instantly around the folded omelet and serve at once. Serves 4.

Sunrise Breakfast for Fifty

The custom of sunrise services on Easter day is a lovely one which is more and more observed. Sunrise on a spring morning can be chilly, though, and worshippers are likely to leave the service cold and hungry and ready for a bang-up breakfast. Another fine custom maintains in many churches where the ladies of the congregation prepare breakfast for as many persons as have indicated interest in coming to the parish house. There is a great variety of dishes which can be offered at such a break-fast. However, I'd like to suggest to you that, though you may have many willing helpers, it's difficult to turn out short-order food for lots of people, even if you're a trained short-order chef. For that reason, I think you should avoid such dishes. Here is a suggestion for a Sunrise Breakfast which is easy to prepare, can stand without harm, and is almost impossible to go wrong with!

Orange Juice *
Creamed Eggs on Ham Slices *
Danish Pastry *
Coffee *

This breakfast is planned to serve fifty. It can be multiplied to any extent you like for a larger crowd.

Orange Juice

12 cans quick-frozen orange juice

Reconstitute the orange juice as near serving time as possible. Don't defrost the juice and use ice water with it. Assign one helper to this job and have her aerate (pour back and forth be-tween two pitchers), a small quantity at a time.

Creamed Eggs

6 dozen hard-cooked eggs
1 pound butter
2 cups flour
4 teaspoons salt

1 teaspoon pepper
4 quarts milk
Paprika

Shell eggs and slice or quarter. Melt butter. Blend in flour smoothly. Add seasonings and milk and cook, stirring constantly, until thickened. Add eggs and stand over hot water until eggs are heated through (at least 15 minutes). Serve over hot ham slices with a sprinkling of paprika on top. (For most amateur cooks, it's easier to make the cream sauce in 2, or even in 4 parts, rather than to try to make the whole quantity at once.)

Ham Slices

9 pounds Ready-to-Eat boned
ham

Have your butcher cut the ham for you into fifty slices. (This amount will give good, 3-ounce slices, which are generous and ample.) Wrap sliced ham in aluminum foil and warm in 300 degree F. oven for an hour or so before serving.

Danish Pastry

Whatever bread-stuff you choose to serve at this breakfast should be bought ready-made. Unless there is a member of your church group who is a perfect fiend for baking, that is! One Danish pastry to a person is quite enough, and they're sufficiently rich not to require butter, which saves a lot of trouble. If you're fortunate enough to live in a town where Greek or Italian Easter bread (with colored eggs baked into its twisted rounds) is available, either makes a delightful addition to the feast. Or you can serve Hot Cross Buns, if you like, though to many of us they stand as a symbol of Good Friday only. In any event, some sort of sweet bread is best because of its not requiring butter.

Coffee

2 pounds coffee	1 pound large cubes of sugar
1 ½ quarts coffee cream	

If you make the coffee from scratch, your 2 pounds will require 5 gallons of water, and this amount will give 50 people 2 cups each. Or, you can use instant coffee, in which case you will need four 2-ounce jars and 5 gallons of boiling water to make the same number of cups.

Breakfast Game

If you long to play a game at breakfast, which some people do, to be sure, try this old Russian one. Have a big bowl of colored hard-cooked eggs on the table. The Russian ones were always those beautifully painted ones in fine, intricate designs, but you can make yours as simple or as elaborate as your humor dictates.

Pass each guest an egg. Each holds his egg in the right hand and, first with the partner on one side, then on the other, attempts to crack the other's egg with his own, which must remain undamaged. There's a trick to keeping one's egg intact, but it's fun to learn. If you crack your opponent's egg it becomes yours and the person who wins most eggs wins the game.

If children are to play this game they need supervision as it is conducive to mild hysteria and upsetting of pretty Easter breakfast tables!

EASTER LUNCHEONS

If you are a dinner-at-night family, you'll want to make something pretty special out of the Easter luncheon hour. And if you're a small family or an only-two-meals-on-Sunday one, you may prefer to make those two a gala luncheon and a light supper. In any case, I offer you here four menus which suggest light, but festive, fare for your Easter midday.

MENU I

Egg Drop Soup *
Ham Slice with Apricots (page 38)
Spinach and Mushrooms *
Melba Toast
Coconut Lamb Cake (page 46)

Egg Drop Soup

2 cans clear chicken broth   1 egg

Heat broth. Beat egg well with fork. Turn into soup and beat until it forms long strings through the soup. Serve at once. Serves 4.

Spinach and Mushrooms

1 package quick-frozen   Butter or margarine
  chopped spinach   ¼ cup cream
½ pound fresh mushrooms   Dash of nutmeg

Cook spinach according to package directions. Meantime, clean mushrooms, chop coarsely and sauté in butter 5 minutes. Add cream. Drain spinach well, stir in mushrooms and cream, and season with nutmeg. Serves 4.

M E N U   I I

Fruit Soup *
Broiled Chicken
New Potatoes with Chives
Green Beans
Russian Kulich, an Easter Bread (page 56)
Brie Cheese and Crackers

Fruit Soup

2 tablespoons quick-cooking   1 package quick-frozen sliced
  tapioca   strawberries, thawed
1½ cups water   1 cup diced fresh orange
Dash of salt   sections
1½−2 tablespoons lemon juice

Combine tapioca and water in saucepan. Cook and stir over medium heat until mixture comes to a boil. Remove from heat. Add salt and lemon juice. Stir to blend. Cool, stirring once after 15-20 minutes. Cover and chill. Before serving, add strawberries and diced orange. Makes 3½ cups or 5-6 servings.

M E N U   I I I

Hot Madrilene
Jellied Ham Mold *
Potato Salad
Hot Hard Rolls
Easter Fluff *

Jellied Ham Mold

1 package lime-flavored gelatin
1 cup hot gingerale
1 cup cold gingerale
2 tablespoons vinegar
½ teaspoon salt

1 cup cooked ham cubes
½ cup chopped celery
¼ cup minced onion
water cress

Dissolve gelatin in gingerale which has been heated, but not boiled. Add cold gingerale, vinegar, and salt. Cool. When slightly thickened, stir in ham, celery, and onion. Pour into melon or ring mold, and chill until firm. Unmold on a bed of water cress, and serve with horse radish Dressing. Serves 4.

Horse-radish Dressing

½ pint heavy cream
2 tablespoons grated horse-

radish
½ teaspoon salt

Whip cream stiff and fold in horse radish and salt. Make just before serving.

Easter Fluff

2 tablespoons gelatin   ½ cup lemon juice
1 cup cold water   2 egg whites
1 cup boiling water   Jelly beans
¼ teaspoon salt   ½ pint heavy cream
½ cup sugar   Green coloring
Grated rind ½ lemon

Soften gelatin in cold water (about 5 minutes). Add boiling water and stir until gelatin has dissolved. Add salt, sugar, lemon rind, and juice. Cool and then chill until gelatin thickens slightly. Beat egg whites until stiff and then beat the gelatin mixture into them. Put into a melon mold and chill until firm. Unmold and decorate with varicolored jelly beans. Whip cream, flavor as desired, and color pale green with vegetable dye. Pile around mold on serving dish. Serves 4-6.

M E N U   I V

Eggs Mayonnaise *
Broiled Lamb Chops
Asparagus with Buttered Crumbs
Hot Buttered Swedish Bread *
Minted Pineapple

Eggs Mayonnaise

4 hard-cooked eggs   2 teaspoons white wine
Water cress   Dash of cayenne
4 tablespoons mayonnaise   Green coloring

Shell eggs and place one on each individual plate in a bed of water cress. Mix mayonnaise, white wine, and cayenne. Color with vegetable dye or spinach juice to a spring green. Pour over eggs. Serve at once. Serves 4.

Hot Buttered Swedish Bread

Butter Swedish bread well. Place in 350 degree F. oven until butter is melted and absorbed and bread heated through.

5

Easter-Day Dinners and Afternoon Parties

For some of us Easter dinner comes in the middle of the day and for others at night. Whenever you serve it, you want to make it one of the most festive and gala occasions of the year. In Chapter 8 on Easter Centerpieces and Favors, you'll find suggestions for decorating the Easter table, whether for breakfast, lunch, or dinner. I have high hopes that you'll add a lot of ingenious ideas of your own and very definitely that you'll let your children help. Easter is a very *family* sort of time and everyone ought to get in on the planning and carrying out of his own family's celebration.

Though, as we've said, ham is the traditional Easter meat,

there are other fine, springlike entrées which you can substitute if you prefer. Here's a variety of menus for your choice.

MENU I

(On frontispiece)

Crown Roast of Pork * Meringue Pear Halves *
Chive Rice * Gravy
Green Beans
Relishes
Daffodil Cake (page 53)

Crown Roast of Pork

Have your butcher prepare a crown of pork. Sprinkle with salt and pepper and dredge with flour. Place a few thin slices of onion here and there on the meat. Place on rack in roasting pan, with a little water in the bottom. Sear 20 minutes in 500 degree F. oven, reduce heat to 300 degrees and roast 45 minutes a pound. Serve surrounded by Meringue Pear Halves, and make gravy from pan drippings.

Meringue Pear Halves

1 egg white
1 tablespoon powdered sugar

1 tablespoon currant jelly, melted

Beat egg white until stiff. Gradually beat in sugar. Add jelly and blend well. Put a teaspoonful of the meringue on each pear half and bake in 300 degree F. oven until lightly browned (about 15 minutes).

Chive Rice

1 ⅓ cups packaged precooked
    rice
1 ½ cups water
  ½ teaspoon salt

2 tablespoons finely chopped
   chives
2 tablespoons butter

Combine rice, water, and salt in saucepan. Mix just until all rice is moistened. Bring quickly to a boil over high heat, uncovered, fluffing gently once or twice with a fork. (*Do not stir.*) Cover and remove from heat. Let stand 10 minutes. Add chives and butter, mixing lightly with a fork. Pile in center of crown roast (if there's extra, serve in a separate dish). Serves 4 or 5.

MENU II

Jellied Chicken Consommé
Baked Ham with Apricot Glaze (pages 33-35)
Sweet Potato Puffs *
Broccoli with Lemon Butter *
Dark Pumpernickel
Lamb Cake (page 46)
Chocolate Ice Cream

Jellied Chicken Consommé

There are so many good examples of this in cans that it seems rather foolish to make your own *unless* you're cooking a stewing chicken anyway. In that case, cook the broth down with bones and bits and extra seasoning to your taste to half its original quantity. Strain well, cool, chill, and remove all fat. Add to the broth (which should be jelled), 1 stiffly-beaten egg white for each 2 cups of broth, and beat this over the heat until it comes to the boil. Allow to stand 10 minutes, then strain through a wet cloth. Chill again.

Sweet Potato Puffs

2 cups mashed sweet potatoes	Pepper and salt
Milk	Dash of nutmeg
1 egg	Crushed cornflakes

After mashing the potatoes, mix with enough milk to make a smooth, but not a bit soft, consistency (very little!). Add egg, beaten, and seasonings. Form into balls about 3 inches in diameter. Flour your hands to do this. Roll in cornflakes. Fry in hot deep fat until golden brown. Drain on absorbent paper. Serves 4.

Lemon Butter

To each ¼ cup of butter, melted, add 1 tablespoonful of lemon juice. Pour over cooked, well-drained broccoli.

MENU II

Mushrooms Vinaigrette *
Roast Veal
Buttered Barley *   Peas Bonne Femme *
Garlic French Bread
Easter Surprise Cake (page 50)

Mushrooms Vinaigrette

1 pound mushrooms	¼ teaspoon salt
1 tablespoon wine vinegar	Fresh ground pepper
3 tablespoons olive oil	1 teaspoon green pepper relish
¼ teaspoon English mustard	1 hard-cooked egg, chopped

Peel and stem mushrooms, and boil them in a very little water about 8 minutes. Drain, cool, and chill. Mix all other ingredients, and pour over individual servings of mushrooms. Serves 4.

Buttered Barley

1 ½ cups barley   Chicken stock
Butter or margarine

Sauté barley in butter or margarine until lightly brown. Cover with chicken stock and simmer gently, adding more stock if necessary, until done (1 ½ – 2 hours). The barley should absorb the stock by the end of its cooking. Serve with melted butter poured over.

Peas Bonne Femme

                     2 tablespoons butter or
4 pounds peas   margarine
8 lettuce leaves   Salt and pepper
1 medium-sized onion

Shell and cook peas. Meantime, shred lettuce and slice onion very thin. Sauté onion in fat until lightly browned; then add lettuce and sauté 3–4 minutes longer, stirring occasionally. When peas are done, drain and mix with onion and lettuce and season to taste with salt and pepper. (This is a highly unorthodox Adams version of Peas Bonne Femme, but delicious, I assure you.)

MENU III

California Salad *
Leg of Spring Lamb
Buttered New Potatoes in Jackets
Asparagus Hollandaise (page 41)
Hard Rolls
Strawberry Shortcake *

California Salad

1 head Boston lettuce	1 teaspoon Worcestershire
1 cup bread cubes	sauce
2 tablespoons garlic-flavored	2 tablespoons grated Parmesan
olive oil	cheese
1 tablespoon lemon juice	2 tablespoons crumbled blue
3 tablespoons olive oil	cheese
Salt and pepper	1 egg

Tear lettuce into serving bowl. Fry bread cubes (crouton-size) in garlic-flavored oil to a golden brown. Drain on absorbent paper. Combine lemon juice, the 3 tablespoons olive oil, salt, pepper, and Worcestershire. Sprinkle cheese over greens. Pour dressing over. Break raw egg over all and toss so that egg causes cheese to coat every leaf. Add croutons and toss again lightly. Serves 4.

Strawberry Shortcake

1 quart strawberries	⅓ cup butter or margarine
Powdered sugar	½ – ¾ cup milk
2 cups flour	½ pint heavy cream
3 teaspoons baking powder	Sugar
2 teaspoons sugar	Vanilla
½ teaspoon salt	

Hull strawberries and wash if necessary. Mash and sprinkle lightly with powdered sugar. Mix and sift dry ingredients. Work in butter or margarine lightly. Add milk gradually. Bake in round pan in 450 degree F. oven 12–15 minutes. Split the cake in two. Butter inside of each half. Place bottom on serving dish. Pour over half the strawberries. Put second half of the cake on top, and pour over the rest of the berries. Whip cream, flavor to taste with sugar and vanilla, and pour over top of cake.

MENU IV

Fruit Cup
Chicken Tarragon *
Brown Rice   Baked Tomatoes *
Clover Rolls
Russian Easter Cake (page 45)

Chicken Tarragon

2 broiler-fryers, cut up	Sprig of tarragon (see note
Seasoned flour	below)
Butter or margarine	Salt and pepper
½ cup white wine	Minced tarragon leaves
1 pint cream	2 egg yolks

Wash chicken pieces and pat dry. Into a brown paper bag put some flour, seasoned with salt, pepper, and paprika. Shake each chicken piece in this flour and sauté in butter or margarine in Dutch oven until golden brown. Add white wine, cream, and tarragon, and simmer gently until chicken is done (about 20 minutes). Remove chicken and discard tarragon sprig. Season to taste with salt and pepper. Add minced tarragon leaves. Beat egg yolks lightly; add a little of the hot sauce and beat. Return to sauce and beat in rapidly and thoroughly. Pour sauce over chicken. Serves 6-8.

Note: If fresh tarragon is not obtainable, try to get the tarragon that comes in a bottle. Otherwise use the dry kind *very sparingly.*

Baked Tomatoes

8 medium-sized tomatoes	1 medium-sized onion, finely
Salt and pepper	chopped
Sugar	Dry bread crumbs
Basil	Butter or margarine

Wash tomatoes, remove stem ends, and cut in half through center. Place, cut-side up, in shallow ovenproof dish. Put in enough water to barely cover the bottom of the dish. Sprinkle each cut-side of tomato with salt, pepper, sugar, basil, and chopped onion. Top generously with bread crumbs, and dot with fat. Bake in 400 degree F. oven until crumbs are brown and tomatoes soft (30-40 minutes). Serves 6-8.

EASTER AFTERNOON PARTIES

Now that the gay season starts, why not ask friends in to celebrate with you in the afternoon? It's an easy sort of party to prepare and serve so that the hosts can have as much fun as their
guests, which is the test of a good party.

You can, of course, make this a tea party or a cocktail party
if you like. But a punch prepared well ahead of time is much the
easiest sort of drink to serve and, if you haven't a big bowl to
serve it in, you should be able to rent one from your local cater-
ing service.

PARTY I

Wine-Fruit Punch *
Cucumber Sandwiches *
Easter Bonnet Cookies (page 54)
Easter Mints

Wine-Fruit Punch

5 bottles sauterne
½ cup lemon juice
1 cup sugar

3 large bottles club soda,
   chilled
3 cups fruit in season
Lots of chopped ice

Mix sauterne with lemon juice and sugar. Let this stand in a bowl
which has been set in a larger bowl filled with ice. When ready
to serve, pour in soda and fruit, mix, and let stand a few minutes
to be sure it's thoroughly cold. Add ice to outer bowl as needed.
Serves 18-20. (Strawberries, pineapple slices, orange and lemon
slices are particularly decorative fruits to use in this punch.)

Cucumber Sandwiches

These should be made on the thinnest possible white bread, so buy the unsliced variety and "sliver" it youself if you can. The cucumber should be sliced paper thin, too. All it really needs is a dash of salt and a grind of fresh pepper, but you may add a suspicion of mayonnaise if you want to. Make approximately 2 half-sandwiches (crusts removed, please) per person.

PARTY II

Eggnog *
Salted Mixed Nuts
Black pumpernickel spread with chive butter
Bowl of pâté with melba toast rounds to spread *

Eggnog

12 egg yolks	3 cups milk
½ cup sugar	3 cups heavy cream
3 cups rye whisky	12 egg whites
1 cup light rum	Nutmeg

Beat egg yolks and sugar until light yellow. Add rye, rum, and milk. Whip cream and fold into first mixture. Beat egg whites until stiff and fold in last. To keep the mixture cold, serve it in a bowl set in a larger bowl filled with ice. Serve with a dash of nutmeg on top of each cupful. This will serve 18-20.

Eggnog is so rich and sweet that it calls for accompaniments which will cut its richness, rather than cake and such. Buy tinned liver pâté and mix it up with a bit of mayonnaise and a dash of brandy. Let the guests spread their own, so there'll be no chance of soggy toast.

PARTY III

Tea Punch *
Thin Chicken Sandwiches
Crystallized Ginger and Orange Peel
Petit Fours

Tea Punch

2 quarts very strong tea
1 ½ quarts grape juice
1 cup sugar (or to taste)
2 cups lemon juice

4 quarts orange juice
2 quarts club soda
Flowers

Mix all ingredients but flowers and chill. If you have a freezer or freezing compartment, fill a container of the size and shape to fit into your punch bowl to within an inch of the top with water, and place in freezer. When almost frozen, make a wreath of Easter flowers, such as daffodils, narcissus, tulips, which you have carefully opened out, and whatever else you'd like, on top of the ice. Fill carefully with water to hold the wreath in place and freeze solid. Place in punch bowl and pour punch over. If you haven't the freezing facilities, float a few flowers in the top of the punch for a lovely effect. Serves about 25.

Petit Fours

Buy them, by all means, from the best pastry shop you know. They're a nuisance to make and can easily turn you into that hostess who's so exhausted she doesn't enjoy her own party, which results in the guests feeling exactly the same way!

PARTY IV

Ginger-Ale Punch *
Liptauer Cheese * Crackers
Tiny Ham Sandwiches *
Raw Vegetables *

Ginger-Ale Punch

2 cups lime juice
2 quarts orange juice
4 quarts gingerale

Sugar to taste
1 quart lime ice

Be sure to chill juices and ginger ale before using. When ready to serve, mix juices and ginger ale and add sugar to taste. Pour over a large block of ice in the punch bowl and float scoops of lime ice on top. Will serve 20-25.

Liptauer Cheese

2 (8-ounce) packages cream
  cheese
½ cup sweet butter
2 tablespoons chopped capers
1 teaspoon salt

1 teaspoon anchovy paste
½ teaspoon minced onion
1 teaspoon dry mustard
1½ teaspoons paprika
Sour cream

Cream the cheese and butter together. Add other ingredients and mix well, using just enough sour cream to make the mixture smooth and spreadable. Chill thoroughly. Serve in a mound decorated with whole capers and paprika, surrounded with crisp crackers.

Raw Vegetables

Offer any variety of these that your fancy dictates or that are
available. There's scarcely a vegetable you can name which isn't
delicious eaten raw. Just as reminders, let me suggest: carrot
curls, celery curls, scallions, radishes, cauliflower, parsnip sticks,
cucumber sticks, plum tomatoes, water cress. Choose for variety
of color, flavor, and texture. All should be icy cold, and all but
the tomatoes should be crisp. For this party, the best accom-
paniment would be a saltcellar of plain salt and one of hickory-
smoked salt. A few artichoke hearts on toothpicks, and some ripe
and green olives might be put on the dishes with them for variety
and color interest.

Tiny Ham Sandwiches

You can probably use some of your leftover Easter ham for
these. Make them on lightly-buttered slices from a little loaf of
salty rye bread. Be sure to have at least one unusual mustard
handy, like Dijon, Chinese, or Bahamian.

6

Parties for Children

EASTER EGG HUNT

From the egg-rolling for hundreds of children on the White House lawn to the family egg-hunt prepared the night before by Mummy and Daddy for their own unbelievably-early-rising young on Easter morn, games about finding Easter eggs have always been the most fun of all at Easter time.

Prizes

If the party is for very little ones, or perhaps even for "middle-aged" school children, it's well to have prizes for almost everybody. Perhaps the eggs themselves, together with the baskets your children have made for collecting them, will be enough of a prize for most of the participants. But everybody loves to win prizes, especially the very little ones who find it quite hard to see why Johnny should have won just because he found four eggs and I only found two. So a generous number of tiny prizes is perhaps better than one or two very splendid ones.

Handicaps

A good idea if ages and abilities among the child-guests vary much is to handicap the older and more competitive. Ages shouldn't vary too widely at a children's party. But sometimes, of necessity and out of real love too, much younger children of the same family must be included. Then fix it, for instance, that anybody eight or nine years old must find two eggs before he begins to count; sixes and sevens must find one; and fives and under can count from the first one found. The older ones will have the compensation of more eggs to carry home. And the little ones will be in the running, despite the handicap of great youth!

Special Eggs

You can have certain eggs marked "Lucky"—just a small percentage of the total hidden. These will rate small prizes and add to the excitement of the hunt.

Outdoors?

Of course it has been known to rain—or even snow!—at the Easter season. But if you live in the country or suburbs and can possibly hide the eggs outdoors, it saves a great deal of wear and tear on your home. The eggs should definitely be hidden by adults. Young hosts like to participate in the games at their own parties, and only if parents do the hiding can they fairly do so. Be careful in hiding the eggs not to make their discovery too difficult for the age that's hunting—not too high above heads, not too buried behind foliage.

Or Indoors?

If you live in a city apartment or house, the hunt must be indoors. And it's quite possible, even if you don't, that there'll have to be a sudden revision of plans due to the March lion or to April showers. One piece of advice here: Try to confine the hunt to one room—two at the most. It's bound to be disruptive to the furniture and the decorative scheme. Remove all small objets d'art which might be knocked over and broken by persons concentrating on, to them, more important matters. When you've made the room as childproof as possible—or put the whole performance into the cellar perhaps—then resolve not to offer a lot of "don'ts" and "carefuls," which will spoil the whole party for you and the guests.

Baskets

Each child should certainly have a basket in which to collect his eggs. The baskets need not be elaborate, but they should definitely be substantial enough so that they won't collapse and cause cracked eggs. If you can find or buy enough strong, small cardboard boxes to go round and provide your child or children with plenty of yellow and green crepe paper, paste, Scotch tape, and whatever he or she feels will be best for extra decoration, *plus* wire which can be wound with paper and then fastened securely to the box, either by wire brads or by putting the handle through the decorated box in some fashion and fastening it securely, the resulting product will be all their own. This is important, and undoubtedly most handsome in the eyes of all young guests.

If your particular egg hunt is based on eggs just dyed by the guests at the party, you may, after each has counted his find, want to redistribute them so that any guest who wants to can carry home the ones he decorated himself. If you think that pride in artistry is likely to run strong, you had better make such an arrangement and hold firmly to it or heartbreak, not to say bloodshed, may result.

If you need extra games to play at a party planned primarily as an egg-hunt, try an egg-race, which consists in carrying hard-cooked eggs (the ones they hunted for can be borrowed back for this), in tablespoons or dessert spoons from a starting line to an Easter basket at the end. Two children play at one time and start the race at a given signal. The one who gets all his eggs into the basket first wins. Eggs dropped on the way are not counted. Fit the distance required from starting line to basket to the age and capabilities of the contestants. For older children, you might make it harder by having them use teaspoons.

"Pin the Tail on the Bunny" is just a seasonal variation of the old favorite, easily made at home. Most children can draw a pretty good bunny outline, with round, fat tail at the bottom, on a piece of muslin provided by Mother. If they want to color or paint it, all the better. Then just have them draw and cut out the required number of duplicate tails to be pinned on.

"WHERE'S THE PARTY?"

People in their school years (and I believe sometimes people many years older), regard the *real* "party" as the food they eat. If you've been a parent even only so long as to have a child who is articulate, you must have had at least one small guest say to you, after your carefully planned games have gone apparently swimmingly for some time, "Mrs. Smith, when is the party?" That means, really, the ice cream and cake. But if you bravely let your own child have a good big hand in deciding what the entire refreshments will be, every child present is likely to be pleased from start to finish.

It is much better, I believe, at any party for children ten and under, to have the refreshments be a meal. If you suddenly provide simply ice cream and cake and candy at five o'clock in the afternoon, as was the custom in my long-distant childhood, and as is sometimes still done today, you destroy appetites for supper and thus spoil the well-rounded nutritional pattern planned for most of today's children.

Soup and sandwiches, followed by the absolutely necessary ice cream and cake, can be entirely adequate for a child's supper party. I know one family of four children whose idea of the most elegant first course possible at a party is tomato soup and bologna sandwiches! The parents tell me in some surprise that most guests seemed to agree entirely! The addition of a few raw vegetables, which most children like, rounds out the meal nutritionally—and then comes the beautiful dessert.

If your neighborhood provides the possibility of purchasing ice cream bunnies, I'm sure you will find them popular with the young guests. However, if you can't get those, "regular" ice cream in bricks will do nicely and you'll fill in the rest of the menu with exceedingly Eastery objects, like chocolate bunnies and chicks, the bunny and chick cupcakes described on page 52 or Jellied Easter Eggs on page 100. On page 60, you will find a recipe for enchanting little Bunny Biscuits which children will love and which you might provide to accompany a salad of cooked vegetables, as a change from the sandwich routine. They could even have bologna with the salad!

There should, of course, be candy cups or containers of some sort on any Easter-party table. Perhaps your children will want to make paper-cup and crepe-paper ones themselves. Here's one, though, which you can make with great ease and which results in having your Easter basket and eating it too!

Candy Easter Nests
(Plate 15)

1 tablespoon butter or margarine (for greasing)	⅓ cup butter or margarine
1 package (about 7 cups) bite-sized shredded rice biscuits	½ pound (about 30) marshmallows
	½ teaspoon vanilla

Butter generously a 4-quart bowl or kettle and 12 custard or coffee cups. Pour bite-sized shredded rice biscuits into buttered bowl. Heat the ⅓ cup butter and marshmallows over boiling water until marshmallows are melted, stirring often to blend. Remove from heat. Stir in vanilla. Pour marshmallow mixture evenly over cereal. Mix with large spoon until all pieces of cereal are coated. Allow to stand 15 to 20 minutes so that mixture is cool and less sticky to handle. Fill each buttered cup ¾ full of cereal mixture. Do not pack.

PLATE 15 CANDY EASTER NESTS

Butter the outside bottom of a fruit juice glass. Using a twisting motion, press it down into the center of the cereal mixture in one cup. With buttered fingers gently pack down the cereal mixture around the sides of the glass. Remove the glass. Butter the glass before shaping each nest. Allow nests to stand over night to become firm. Loosen sides from cups with small knife and remove. Fill with candy eggs or jelly beans. Makes 12 nests, 3 inches wide and 1½ inches high.

Decorating the Party Table

As for table decorations for the children's Easter party, the major point is that the young hosts should concoct them themselves. Give them plenty of crepe paper, cardboard, Scotch tape, shredded green cellophane (for grass or nests), and let them go their own gait. If a Jack Horner pie seems in order, look over our Easter Hen on page 116 and let the children have a hand in its making.

7

Easter Eggs to Dye
or Make

Easter eggs take many forms, but whichever you may choose, they are the most deeply traditional part of the children's Easter celebrations.

Dye Them

Dying eggs is probably the most fun of all. It can be either a huge headache for the mother of the family, or a good time for everyone. Realistic planning is what brings the latter result. Egg-dying can be very messy and is inevitably somewhat so. It is probably best done in the kitchen, but perhaps the cellar or the back porch will seem more suitable to you. A good pile of news-papers to spread on floor, table, counter space, or wherever any-one is going to work begins the saving of mess. A good collection of metal or plastic bowls for holding various colors comes next. After that, perhaps the next most important item is coveralls for every dyer.

Use only pure food egg dyes and follow instructions on the package.

Egg-Dying Party

You can make a children's Easter party simply by inviting the guests to come and dye eggs. In that case, see that each guest brings his own smock or overalls, and even so does not wear "best" clothes. It doesn't take long for the eggs to dry, and an adult can be present for the express purpose of hiding them for a hunt later on.

Hard-cooked eggs are certainly the easiest to dye. You may help your littlest to learn more complicated ways of decorating eggs if you want to, but certainly for an egg-dying party the hard-cooked kind are the only possible choice.

Those little metal holders for gripping the eggs when dying are a boon, and not expensive. If you're having a large party and can't see much point in providing one for every guest, simply acquire several and let people take turns. With these holders, it is much easier to dye an egg in several stripes, or perhaps to trickle one color over another after the first has dried.

Decorate Them
(Plate 16)

Some children love to paint eggs with a fine-pointed paintbrush. For this type of artistry, water-color paints are probably best, though it can be done with dyes. I feel that this sort of egg-decoration ought to be encouraged. Who knows, you might one day produce an egg-painter to rival the Ukrainians! But it also seems to me something for individual home effort, not to be done in the midst of a situation as social as an egg-dying party.

For party or just by-yourself decorating, gummed signal dots offer splendid and infinite possibilities for making eggs gay. Crepe paper enables you to make hats, bunny ears, and other decorations. Or you can cover the egg entirely with it—and decorate from there. Silver "flitter" is lovely to sprinkle on lightly-spread paste to make a glittery egg. Lace doilies, notorial seals, colored Scotch tape, little flower seals—all offer great help to the imaginative egg-decorator.

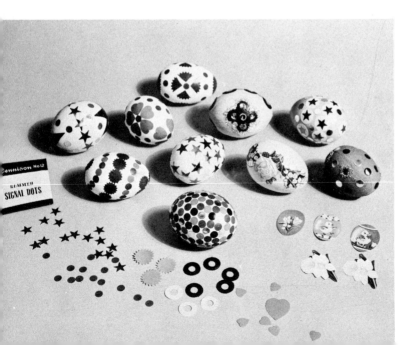

PLATE 16

DECORATED

EASTER EGGS

Blow Them

Of course, all the beautiful Ukrainian and Russian Easter eggs are blown. This is not nearly as hard as it sounds. But after it's done, the eggs must be handled with great care, as they're exceedingly fragile. To blow them, prick a pin hole in each end. Push the pin in gently, being careful not to crack the egg, then work it in a little to make the hole big enough (still tiny). Now take a deep breath and blow through one end. The egg will slip quite easily through the other end. (Be prepared to make a lot of cake as soon as you've finished blowing!)

If you're going to decorate blown eggs, it's a good plan to have some little paper nut cups to set them in while working on them, and perhaps to use as standards for them later. You can also make standards out of very heavy paper.

Ready-Made

There are now available plastic Easter egg halves which can be put together to make a whole egg (six halves come in a sheet). These can be clipped or pushed out of the sheet in which they come, filled with candy or a little favor, and threaded with ribbon or cord to form the whole egg. They can also be decorated with stickers for further gaiety. They cost about 50 cents for a sheet of 6 halves.

There is also a large plastic "picture-window" egg, the top half of which, viewed through a peephole shows a colorful Easter scene in three dimensional relief, while the lower half is a hollow, easy-to-fill candy container. These cost about $2.50, so can hardly be regarded as party favors, but might make a pleasant

Easter-morning surprise for your own child. They're not, to be sure, equipped with that wonderful crusty, sugary-looking outside that some of us remember with joy from our own childhood, which seem almost to have disappeared completely. But they're less breakable, and perhaps will do the same pleasant thing for our children that the old ones did for us.

Jellied Easter Eggs
(Plate 17)

1 package fruit-flavored gelatin   ½ cup cold water
   (any flavor)   8 egg shells
1 cup hot water

To remove yolks and whites from egg shells, crack small end of each egg slightly. Pick away enough shell so that the yolk and white will drop out. Rinse inside of shell with cold water.

PLATE 17   JELLIED EASTER EGGS

Dissolve gelatin in *hot water*. Add cold water. Pour into egg shells, using funnel or small pitcher. Set eggs on end in egg container and chill over night.

Dip "eggs" quickly in warm water, crack shells, and peel off. Serve gelatin eggs in nests made of shredded lettuce or coconut. Using pastry tube, decorate with whipped cream or cream cheese (softened and flavored, if desired), making designs or spelling out initials or children's names. Makes 8 Easter eggs.

Coconut Easter Eggs

2 cups sugar	1 teaspoon vanilla
Dash of salt	1½ cups shredded coconut
2 tablespoons light corn sirup	6 squares candy-making chocolate, melted
1¼ cups water	

Combine sugar, salt, corn sirup, and water. Place over low heat and stir constantly until sugar is dissolved and mixture boils. Cover and cook 3 minutes; then remove cover and continue boiling, without stirring, until a small amount of sirup forms a soft ball in cold water (or to a temperature of 238 degrees F.). During cooking, wash down sides of pan occasionally with damp cloth. Pour fondant at once on cold wet platter or marble slab or on greased surface. Cool to lukewarm (110 degrees F.). Work with paddle or spatula until white and creamy. Add vanilla and knead until smooth. Store in covered jar to ripen for several days.

Add shredded coconut to fondant. Knead and form into egg shapes. Set on lightly-buttered tray until firm. Using a toothpick, dip coconut eggs in chocolate, coating entire surface.

8

Easter

Centerpieces and Favors

Easter decorations are easy and fun to produce. Whether you're having a party or not, this time of year cries out for the use of spring blossoms, pussy willows, and delicate green leaves.

Flowers

In making Easter floral centerpieces, do try to keep them simple. Daffodils, freesias, narcissus, snapdragons, tiny sweetheart roses, acacia—and any other flowers which spell spring in your part of the country—need little embellishment beyond their own simple beauty to make a stunning table decoration. Green, yellow, and white are perhaps the most "Eastery" colors, but pink is spring-like too and you may, if you like, mix in any of the pastels you can find. Pastel colors mix with each other beautifully, so if you're tired of sticking to a one-color theme, try using as many different colors as you can get.

Of course, for a party, you'll probably want to carry the decorations farther than just the flowers, though at a formal dinner party for adults you can make the table complete and lovely by placing a simple little nosegay (perhaps in a paper frill), at each lady's place, repeating the flowers used in the centerpiece. Boutonnieres for the men are fun, too, if the flowers you're using happen to include any which are appropriate for them to wear.

"Egg Candles"

An additional gay and festive note can be added to a beautiful Easter dinner table by egg-shaped candles which you decorate yourself. Some of the most exclusive shops showed these last year, at exceedingly high prices, but you can turn them out with very little trouble or expense and a lot of fun. They come in aqua, yellow, and green—egg-shaped, as I said, and with one end cut off for them to stand on. Simply get paper stars and other stickers, also sequins and/or any small millinery decorations you can pick up. There are some such which come with very short pins through the centers, and they are fine for decorating the candles.

Make set designs, if you like, or just scatter your decorations with abandon. The end result is charming, in any case, and gives rather the effect of elaborately painted Ukrainian Easter eggs! If you don't find the candles easily in your local shops, they are made by the Emkay Candle Studios, 225 Fifth Avenue, New York 10. Write them for information on the nearest shop where you can buy the candles.

If you use these candles on an informal dinner or buffet table you might decorate colored paper napkins more or less to match. They are gay and exceedingly effective!

Place Cards
(Plate 18)

You can do practically all your decorating, except for the center-piece, by way of place cards, if you like. Children will love them and they're really equally appropriate for adult parties. We have illustrated some easy-to-make egg-shell place cards on page 105. First, save your broken egg shells when you bake the Easter cake. Here's how to put the place cards together.

Tulip: Tint half of a broken egg shell and paste it to a place card. Tint 5 toothpicks green and paste 2 green crepe paper leaves to each. Stick varicolored jelly beans on the top of each. Stick all 5 into a gumdrop, and place it inside the egg shell.

Sailboat: The eggs for these should be broken lengthwise, with one half much larger than the other. Use the larger half for a "boat." Cut a sail from crepe paper and paste it to a pipe cleaner. Put the other end of the pipe cleaner through the bottom of the shell and into a gumdrop to hold the boat steady. Trim the boat with lines of twisted crepe paper—and be sure to put a star on the sail! Then fill the boat with jelly beans, and set the gum-drop on your place card.

Easter Flower: Tint half of a broken egg shell yellow. Cut a strip of 6 petals from yellow crepe paper, and paste it around the bottom of the egg, curling the petals with your thumb. Paste the egg to a place card and trim the flower with a ribbon bow. Fill the egg with jelly beans.

You can also make enchanting place cards out of whole blown eggs. Use them as "heads," and make bonnets for them out of crepe paper or bits of lace, embroidery, ribbon, and cloth. You might trim some of the bonnets with real flowers. Either tint white eggs flesh color for this or use pale brown ones. Make features with bits of colored paper—black for eyelashes (you can make very coy faces without adding eyes at all, just downcast lashes!), red for mouths, blue for eyes. And put each finished egg into a "collar" of cardboard, to which you attach the place card, so it can stand easily.

PLATE 18 PLACE CARDS

Rabbit Centerpiece

If you happen to be the happy possessor of one or more of those enchanting little English porcelain rabbits with pink clover blossoms all over them, or if you feel inclined to make yourself an Easter present of a pair, you can make a beguiling centerpiece based on them. Get flowers as near the color of their clover blossoms as possible. Then scatter them around the rabbits in a very shallow bowl—or on a mirror.

Ducks and Chicks

Many people of my generation remember with great nostalgia the little stuffed chicks and ducks which always greeted us on the dining table Easter morning. They're to be had again now in many places, and they afford a wonderful base for a really Eastery table. They can be placed in shredded green cellophane "nests"—or they can walk on a "lawn" of the same material and they are the delight of small fry. To me, Easter isn't Easter without them, chocolate bunnies notwithstanding!

Bunny Napkin-Holder

If you can make even the simplest freehand drawing you can do this, and the children will love it. On thinnish white cardboard, draw a rabbit about 5″ high, from the tip of his standing-up ears to his feet. At his base, draw some solid pieces out to each side which can be creased back to make him stand up. Have his "arms" out to each side and when you cut him out, paste them together and slip a folded paper napkin through them. Draw any kind of gay and smiling face you like.

Marshmallow Bunny

Here's an edible favor for a children's party, which your young can very likely make themselves. It's just a bunny head made out of a marshmallow, on the flat side of which you make features with tiny blobs of differently-colored frosting. Then make ears out of white crepe paper, lined with pink, stuck on with frosting. Set the head in a frilly paper collar—and decorate in front of one ear with a ribbon bow—very jaunty!

Chicken in Nest

You can use blown eggs for this, or hard-cooked ones, which will be a part of the children's supper or everybody's lunch! Whichever you decide on, color the egg yellow. Buy packaged chick heads and tails at your local stationer's—they're made by Dennison. Stick them on the egg to make a chick. Now make a nest for the chick to sit in, out of twisted, pale-green crepe paper —and glue the chick to it.

Easter-Bunny Centerpiece
(Plate 19)

Materials needed: White, green, and pink crepe paper, gummed tape, paper towels, cotton, mat stock, spool wire, paste.

To make the *body*, cut a half circle of mat stock, 14″ in radius, and roll it into a cone (Fig. A). Fasten with paper fasteners or gum tape. To make the *head*, crush and roll paper towels to shape head, 4″ deep and 3″ across. Wind with a 1″ strip of crepe paper, paste, and stretch crepe as you wind. Cut a hole in the bottom of the head with a sharp knife, paste end of body, and stick the head on it (Fig. A).

To make the *arms*, turn 1″ back on either end of 18″ length of wire, and wind with ½″ strip of white crepe paper as in Fig. B.

For *sleeve*, cut strip of pink crepe paper, 18″ with grain, and 10″ across. Paste to form a tube, 18″ long, and slip over "arms." Gather sleeve at either end and fasten at wrists (Fig. C).

For the *blouse*, cut a strip of pink crepe paper 12″ with the grain and 16″ across. Fold in half, making a double strip 6″ deep. Place fold over knitting needle and gather crepe paper as shown in Fig. D.

PLATE 19   EASTER-BUNNY CENTERPIECE

Draw twine together as in Fig. E.

Bring twine around bunny's neck and tie firmly in place on one side as in Fig. F. Make a slit from the open edge to 1″ from gathered edge on the opposite side of the blouse for the other armhole. Pad the front slightly with cotton to give a full-bosomed effect. Place the arms in the back of the body under the blouse (Fig. F). Gather the blouse at the waist and secure it (Fig. F).

The *skirt* is a strip of green crepe paper, the full width of the crepe and 36″ long. Fold the strip in half, gather, and tie it at the waist, just as you fastened the blouse.

The *apron* is a strip of white crepe paper 9″ with the grain and 12″ across. Turn back a 3″ cuff, making the finished apron 6″ deep. Seam the cuff at the sides and center, to make two pockets (Fig. G). A strip of crepe paper 2″ wide and 14″ long makes the *apron strings*. Fold both edges of the strip into the center, then in half (as in bias binding). Gather the apron top with needle and thread and paste the strip over the gathers, centering it so the ties will be of equal length. Tie in a bow in back (Fig. G).

Paste a thin layer of cotton over the entire head to simulate *fur*. Make bunny *eye, ear, nose,* and *mouth* patterns. Cut eyes from dark blue paper and nose and mouth from red. Paste in place. Cut ears from pink crepe paper, backed with letter paper (Fig. H), and cover letter-paper side with a thin layer of cotton (Fig. I).

Let ears dry thoroughly before pinning in place on head (Fig. J) with common pins. Cover the pinheads by pulling a bit of the cotton over them.

Paste whiskers of thread in place under the nose.

Draw large bunny *foot* on construction paper and cut out.

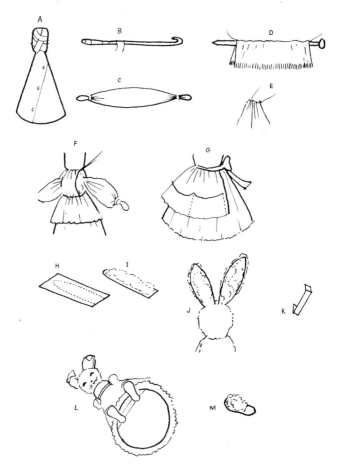

EASTER-BUNNY CENTERPIECE – STEP-BY-STEP

Cut a 1″ strip of construction paper long enough to go across the bottom of the body, 1″ from the front and turn over the edges 1″ (Figs. K and L). Tape or glue in place as in Fig. L. Cover two-thirds of bunny feet with cotton (Fig. M), and glue to strip under body as in Fig. L.

Easter-Basket Centerpiece and Chick Favor
(Plate 20)

Materials Needed: Yellow and orchid crepe paper, #15 and spool wire, Dennison Chick and Bunny cut-outs, white lightweight cardboard, 10″ paper plate, La France bead-bluing, dyed egg shells, glue, flowers, and ribbon.

Cut yellow crepe paper across the grain 5″ wide and 30″ long, and fold it in half lengthwise. Paste one end of the strip over a 10″ paper plate, stretching the paper around to bind the plate. Cut away the surplus paper and paste the strip down.

Wrap separately 2 29″ pieces of #15 wire with orchid crepe paper cut across the grain 1″ wide. Rewrap the wire several times for thickness, bend it, and fasten the ends 1″ apart to the underside of the plate with cellophane tape.

Cut a strip of lightweight cardboard 2″ wide and long enough to go around the plate. Cut a strip of yellow crepe paper 4½″ wide through the fold, open, and refold into 8 layers. Hold in place with pins and fringe both sides, leaving 2″ in the center uncut (Fig. A).

Brush the tips of the fringed crepe paper with Easter Blue, which is made by pouring a cup of La France bead-bluing into a small deep bowl, adding ¼ cup of cold water, and beating with an egg beater into a creamy consistency. Let dry.

A
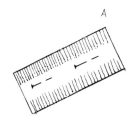

B
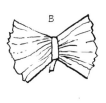

TECHNIQUE FOR EASTER BASKET AND CHICK FAVOR

Paste fringed strip to the cardboard band, gathering it as you go, and allowing the fringe to extend over both sides. Paste the band together and slip it over the plate. Fasten to the handles with cellophane tape. Bend fringe out around the bottom.

Paste chick and bunny cut-outs around the basket and trim the handle with a large ribbon bow and flowers.

PLATE 20 EASTER-BASKET CENTERPIECE AND CHICK FAVORS

Chick Favor

Cut a strip of yellow crepe paper 1½″ wide through the fold, using about 24″ for each chick body. Open each strip and refold it into 8 layers. Hold in place with pins, and fringe both sides leaving 1″ uncut in the center (Fig. A, page 111).

Gather each strip through the center, rolling as you gather, tie with spool wire (Fig. B, page 111). Cut strips 1″ x 12″ for heads, and fringe them in the same way. Tie heads and bodies together, leaving about 1″ stem.

Paste eyes and beak in place. Attach chick to one end of a piece of lightweight cardboard, cut into an egg shape; bind with a ½″ strip of colored crepe paper, folded in half and stretched around it. Dye egg-shell halves, glue them to the other ends of the cardboards, and fill with small candies. Write names along the front of the cardboard.

Miss Bunny Centerpiece
(Plate 21)

Materials Needed: 1 fold each of pink, white, light blue, yellow, and Nile-green crepe paper, pink duplex, #15 wires, 3 #10 wires, spool wire, 1 mailing tube, writing paper, cotton, lace-paper doilies, heavy cardboard, white mat stock, paste, and ribbon.

Legs: Cut 2 10″ lengths of heavy wire. Bend each back for 1″ at one end. Cut 2 ovals 2¾″ x 1¾″ from heavy cardboard for soles and tape bent ends of wire to them to make feet.

Cut two 7″ lengths from mailing tube, and slip over wires for legs. Wind the remaining 16″ length of heavy wire several times with a ½″-wide strip of white crepe paper, cut across the grain.

Bend wire to form a U-shape, and tape one end to each heel, making a standard to hold Miss Bunny erect. Pad toes with tissue to form the feet. Cover the mailing tube legs with a layer of white cotton, seamed together with needle and thread.

Shoes: Cut a strip of blue crepe paper 7″ wide with the grain, and 6″ across for each shoe. Fold strip in half (3½″ x 6″), and fold open edge back for ½″. Starting at standard wire, back of foot, stretch each strip around a foot, pasting the folded edge under the sole of the shoe. Paste a ½″ seam at the back of the shoe. Cut a second set of soles from white wrapping paper, and paste them over the bottoms of the shoes. Tie white ribbon bows around the ankles.

Head: Crush tissue paper to form a ball 12″ in circumference. Tie two 18″ lengths of #10 wire around the ball, twisting all 4 ends together at the base of the head, leaving the surplus free below the head. Attach 2 wire ends to each leg wire, and cover the head and wires with cotton, seaming with a needle and thread. Wind space between the head and legs with a 1″-wide strip of white crepe paper to make the body.

Arms: Crush two sheets of tissue the long way and wind to a 16″ length of #15 wire with a 1″ strip of white crepe paper. Cover with a layer of white cotton and seam together with a needle and thread. Fasten the arms to the body with spool wire.

Ears: Cut two ears, 9″ long and 3″ wide at the widest point from pink duplex. Paste a length of #10 wire down the center of each ear and cover each with a thin layer of cotton. Paste or stitch around the edge of the ear to hold the cotton in place. Sew in place.

Features: Cut eyes and nose from pink duplex, outline in black and paste in place. Cut 4″ lengths of white spool wire for whiskers, bend in half, and paste in place.

PLATE 21   MISS BUNNY CENTERPIECE

Clothes: Make dress and panties of pink crepe paper, trimmed with white crepe-paper ruffles and ribbon bows. Hat is a 4″ circle of white mat stock, covered with yellow crepe paper, trimmed with flowers, made from pink, blue, and yellow crepe paper and ribbon bows. More crepe paper flowers tied with a ribbon bow and placed in the center of a lace-paper doily make a fetching bouquet for Miss Bunny to carry.

Easter Hen Jack Horner Pie

Materials Needed: Azure-blue, grass-green, light-yellow, and red crepe paper; spool wire, lightweight cardboard, 10″ paper plate, paste, and green tape.

Hen: Cut 2 hens from lightweight cardboard, following pattern Fig. A. Cut tabs on bottom and bend forward. Stretch fully and crush an 18″ square of azure-blue crepe paper, and smooth out slightly. Brush paste over entire hen and apply crushed crepe paper, pressing in place. Cover other piece the same way, making sure crepe-paper-covered sides face out. Trim neatly and put under heavy books to dry flat.

Cover comb and beak with red crepe paper. Paint in eyes. Paste the edges of the two hens together along top of head and down front and back as indicated in Fig. A. When dry, place on back of 10″ paper plate that has been covered with crushed green crepe paper. Spread center of hen apart about 3″ and hold tabs to plate with gummed tape.

Cut a strip of green crepe paper through the fold 2½″ wide. Open and refold into 8 layers, pin together, and cut into fringe 2″ deep. Paste around plate 2″ from rim, gathering slightly as you go. Add 2 more rows to cover plate. Make about 14 flowers and plant around base by inserting stem through plate and fastening to underside of plate with gummed tape.

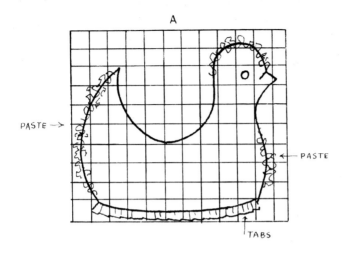

A

PASTE →

← PASTE

TABS

GRAIN OF CREPE

B

8"

12"

C

PATTERN FOR EASTER HEN JACK HORNER PIE

Flowers: Cut flower pattern from yellow crepe (Fig. B). Fold on dotted line and insert 5″ piece of spool wire. Push together tightly, twist wire, and spread flower into shape (Fig. C). Cut leaves and wrap to wire stem with green crepe paper. Fill hen with shredded green crepe paper. Add favors, tied to ribbons long enough to reach each guest's place.

Easter Egg Jack Horner Pie

Cut a piece of cardboard in egg shape—about 12″ the long way. Pile crumpled crepe paper on it (a bit of glue to hold the bottom layer to the cardboard will help), to form an egg shape. Place tiny favors, wrapped and attached to long ribbons, in amongst the crumpled crepe paper and bring all ribbons down to the cardboard—then streaming out.

Cover the crumpled crepe paper with smooth crepe paper, pasting it down where the ribbons *aren't*. Decorate the "egg" with star, rabbit, or whatever kind of sticker you like. When the ribbons are pulled at table, the egg will be broken to bits.

Part II

EASTER GIFTS

9

Easter Baskets

One of the charming and thoroughly traditional Easter customs is that of carrying baskets filled with flowers, Easter eggs, or personal presents large or small to one's friends. These can be baskets you make yourself from scratch or "boughten" ones.

We have lived for the past several years in a basket-mad world, and quite logically so. There are so many beautiful baskets to be had in every size, shape, and color and at any price from pennies to a good many dollars, that anyone who wants a basket can find exactly the one her heart desires with a minimum of research. All these baskets—large and small—make ideal starters toward achieving exactly the right Easter touch to hold what-

ever gift you have in mind. In fact, frequently, the basket itself
can be the major gift. However, it should always be filled in
proper Easter tradition.

If you can ascertain what are the flowers on your best friend's
Easter bonnet, you might buy her one of the little basket "hand-
bags" in natural or painted straw and decorate it with flowers
to match the ones on her hat. This can certainly be done for a
member of the family whose bonnet plans you've probably dis-
cussed at length!

The heavy straw hampers, in which food and wine are often
presented, make wonderful week-end carrying cases of practically no weight. You might fill one of these with home-grown
flowers, the lid tied open with an Easter ribbon of pale green
and yellow. Or choose a tiny gift like a pair of earrings, and hide
it away in masses of slightly crumpled crepe paper in many
colors—*neatly crumpled,* you understand, not just messed up!
These hampers are ideal gifts for passionate picnickers, and
another thing you might fill yours with for such a group is
plastic or paper dinnerware for their outdoor eating.

For a shut-in friend or relative, you might outfit an Easter
basket with a variety of gifts—a book, a jar of your own best
homemade jam, some very special crackers, and a game, for
instance. With gifts like these, the main point is to think hard
about the person to whom you will give it and try to fit his way
of living and thinking. Thoughtfulness is much more important
than money spent.

For a little girl, you might choose a very small basket, which
she can later use as a purse. If it has no lid, make it a drawstring
top of material which will match her Easter outfit. Inside, you
might put an artificial flower to pin on her lapel.

If your children want to give Easter baskets to each other or to older friends, encourage them to make these themselves. If you've given them lots of practice and encouragement in their earliest years, by the time they're eight or ten they should be able to cope with the whole situation themselves without further help from you.

However, the parents who thus aid their children are rare, so if your young seem relatively helpless about the whole matter, here are some suggestions for baskets they might make. If they have original ideas of their own which they wish to incorporate, please don't discourage them even though they may not meet your ideal of perfect taste and/or workmanship! And if you choose one of the more complicated ones, make it—and give it —yourself!

Rose Basket

Materials Needed: Small rectangular box, strip of mat stock, light-pink and leaf-green crepe paper, spool wire.

First cover outside of box with pink crepe paper. Wrap a strip of mat stock (½″ x 14″) with a ½″-wide strip of pink crepe paper, and paste ends to inside of basket to form handle. Cut a 2½″-wide strip of pink crepe paper across the fold (Fig. A).

Cut off a 42″-long strip. Refold it and cut 1½″-deep slits every 1½″ (Fig. B).

Cut these sections into petals shaped as shown. Cup each petal through center (Fig. C).

Cut off 10 petals for roses (below). Cut remaining petal strip in half. Paste one row of petals up near the top, the other row a little lower. Cut a 1½″-wide strip of green crepe paper across the fold. Cut off a 16″-long piece. Fold it and cut 1″-deep fine slashes along one edge. Paste around bottom of box.

Roses: Using a section of the petal strip (5 petals), roll them around each other (Fig. D), and tie tightly at bottom with spool wire, leaving 4″-long ends (Fig. E).

Take a bit of the finely-slashed green crepe paper and paste it around the rose for a calyx. Wrap stem with a ½″-wide strip of green crepe paper, adding small leaves of green as you wind (Fig. F). Make two roses and wire them to the handle of the basket.

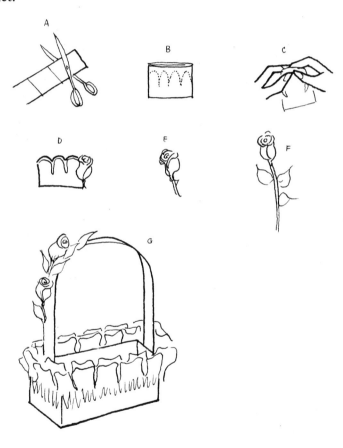

ROSE BASKET – STEP-BY-STEP

Easter Bonnet Baskets

Materials Needed: Pink mat stock; cold-drink cups; Scotch tape; 4″ lace-paper doilies; pink, yellow, light-blue, and spring-green crepe paper; paste; 2 yards ½″ white ribbon; spool wire.

To Make: Cut cup down to 2″ height. Cut bonnet brim, as illustrated, from pink mat stock. Cut a circle of the pink mat stock to fit over the bottom of the cup. Tape this to cup with Scotch tape. Cut 2½″-wide strip of pink crepe paper across the fold. Brush the cup foundation with paste. Stretch crepe-paper strip once around the cup foundation, allowing crepe paper to roll in ¼″ at both top and bottom of cup to cover edge and crown where taped. Paste brim around crown and bind it with a ½″-wide strip of pink crepe paper.

Cut tiny, ½″-wide, flat flowers from yellow and blue crepe paper and flat leaves from spring-green crepe paper. Paste 7 of the flowers, with 4 leaves, along the front of the brim.

Make slits in the crown of the hat on each side. Run a 14″ length of ribbon through the slits, allowing 2″ to emerge on each side. The remainder forms a handle for the basket. Divide the rest of the ribbon in half and make a looped bow from each piece. Fasten bows with spool wire and paste one over each slit.

HOW TO MAKE EASTER BONNET BASKET

Flowers 'n' Lace

Materials Needed: Small square box; six 5″ lace-paper doilies; 1 yard each of yellow and light green ¼″ ribbon; enough orchid wrapping paper to cover the box; pink, yellow, blue, and spring-green crepe paper; paste.

To Make: Place a small gift inside the box. Wrap the box with orchid paper. Paste one doily to each wide side of the box. Paste two more doilies, gathered in center, to center of first doilies. Cut tiny oval flower petals (2 of each color), from pink, blue, and yellow crepe paper, and cut 6 rather long narrow leaves from spring green. Paste 1 set of each color petal and 3 leaves in the center of each set of gathered doilies.

Tie both green and yellow ribbon around narrow side of box so that the tying will come at the top. Allow double 7″ ends of ribbon to remain for handles. Make a looped bow of both shades of ribbon, and tie to top of ribbon handles.

Children in certain parts of Sweden have a charming custom of giving each other Easter baskets, accompanied always by paintings appropriate, in their opinion, to the receiver. Many of these turn out to be cartoonlike in quality, others sweetly serious. Children who are not over-critically handled in these respects love to paint and draw and thoroughly enjoy one another's efforts in this direction. Do encourage yours to produce original art work to accompany their gifts!

10

About Easter Pets

Every year the ASPCA makes a tremendous effort to dissuade people from giving baby chicks and ducks and bunnies to children as Easter presents. Being a complete advocate of their point of view, I cannot in good conscience put down anything in this book regarding Easter pets except a plea that you do not give them.

Little children—and that means boys and girls pretty well up into school age—may dearly love these tiny, soft, live presents when they first arrive. Some will love them so much that it's *too* much for the baby creatures. Too much handling, squeezing, and fondling is more than they can take. Then frequently if they survive the loving-care period, neglect sets in. Most parents, except on farms, are not prepared to take care of such live stock. Often these Easter "pets" die of starvation or manage to run away to who knows what fate within a week or two.

Few children under eight, and a good many up to ten, are not capable of the sustained responsibility of caring for pets of any kind. This should not be held against the children. They should simply not be put into the position of carrying a burden beyond their years. In any case, if children are to have pets, especially if the children are very young, those pets should be creatures of a size, if not age, able to cope with the rough (though perhaps loving), handling and pranks which are natural to the youngsters, and which they might better practice on each other!

I think most parents will be relieved to accept the ASPCA point of view on this matter. Even on farms, while children may be delighted to watch and learn about baby animals, these should be part of the total farm population—and not the personal *property* of any child.

If by any misfortune, despite your own good intentions and efforts, Easter pets arrive unexpectedly at your house, call the ASPCA for advice on what to do about them, both immediately and eventually. They'll be glad to cooperate in your humanitarian efforts.

Easter is a time of love and kindness. Let's make it so for animals, as well as for our young.

11

Gifts to Make for Children

ABBREVIATIONS

General

dec	decrease
inc	increase
incl	inclusive
st(s)	stitch(es)
"	inch(es)
*	asterisk—Repeat the instructions following the asterisk as many times as specified, in addition to the original.

Crocheting

ch	chain
dc	double crochet
half dc	half double crochet
rnd(s)	round(s)
sc	single crochet
sdc	short double crochet
sl st	slip stitch
tr	treble
trc	triple crochet

Knitting

d.p.	double-pointed
k	knit
p	purl
psso	pass slip stitch over
sl	slip
tog	together

Tatting

ch	chain
cl	close
d	double stitch
LR	large ring
p	picot
r	ring
sep	separated

TOYS TO MAKE

Since I hope so much that you will agree with me about not giving live pets as Easter presents, I give you here several bunnies and a chick which you can sew and/or crochet for youngsters. They are equally cuddly and offer the added advantage of being insensitive to pain and unobjecting to any kind of treatment!

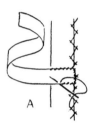

Rabbit
(Plate 22)

Materials Needed: ¼ yard terry cloth or towel or plain muslin: scraps of percale; cotton batting; J. & P. Coats or Clark's O.N.T. Six Strand Embroidery Floss. J. & P. Coats or Clark's O.N.T. Mercerized Sewing Thread.

To make patterns actual size, transfer diagrams as shown to large paper marked with ½″ squares. One small square equals one ½″ square.

Directions for Making: From pattern cut as many of each as indicated—all from terry cloth except two of the ear pieces (percale).

Allow ⅜″ around all edges for seams.

Mark joining lines on body and head with running stitches.

1. Stitch both body pieces together, leaving top open. Turn. Stuff.

2. For each arm or leg, stitch 2 arm or leg pieces together around outer edge, leaving top edge open.

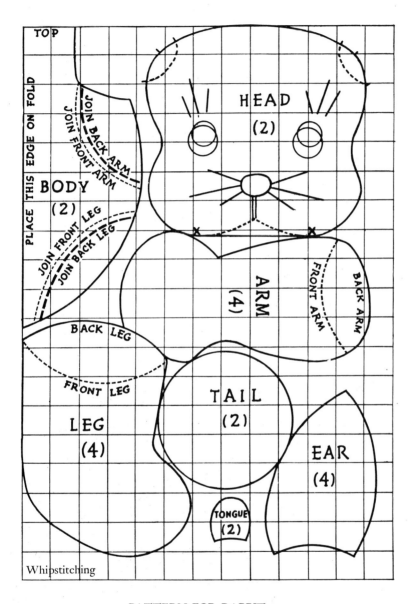

PATTERN FOR RABBIT

3. Stuff to within ⅜″ of top edge. Turn under ⅜″ and fit to body on marked lines, adjusting stuffing. Whip in place by taking small over-and-over stitches close together through both thicknesses. Be sure to make stitch short or fabric will pucker up when it is pulled tight (see Fig. A).

4. Stitch tail pieces together, leaving small opening. Turn, stuff, whip opening together and stitch to back between legs.

5. Stitch tongue around curved edge, turn, stuff. Stitch head pieces together, leaving opening between x marks, and turn. Stuff and stitch head to neck as in step 3. Turn front under on dotted line and insert tongue, tipping head before whipping down.

6. Stitch one terry ear to one percale ear around curved edge. Turn. Turn in raw edges and whip to back of head along marks.

7. Cut out eye and nose pieces, allowing just enough to turn under, and appliqué in place, or embroider features. Make French knots evenly spaced to cover body.

8. Cut a strip of percale 1½″ x 13″. Fold lengthwise, stitch along edge, turn, press and tie around neck.

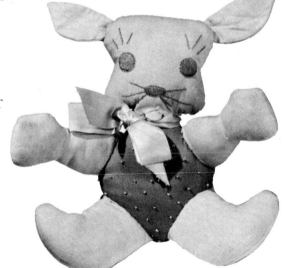

PLATE 22   RABBIT

Easter Chick
(Plate 23)

Materials Needed: 2 balls brown and 1 ball yellow (1-ounce balls) of Chadwick's Red Heart Knitting Worsted; 1 ball each of red and yellow J. & P. Coats or Clark's O.N.T. Pearl Cotton, size 5; No. 5 and No. 1 plastic crochet hooks; 2 star sequins for eyes.

For key to abbreviations, see page ooo.

Pompon Body: Cut 2 circles of cardboard, each 4″ in diameter. Then cut a circle 2″ in diameter at center of each circle. Place one cardboard circle on top of the other. * Cut 4 strands of brown, each about 4 yards long. Draw one end of these strands through center of circle from back, pass them over outer edge and draw them through center of circle again (thus covering cardboard). Continue in this manner until yarn is all used up. Repeat from * until center of circle is completely filled in, using yellow strands of yarn every now and then to form light spots. With sharp scissors or razor cut yarn between the 2 cardboard circles at outer edge. Cut 2 strands of brown about 10″ long. Double these strands and slip between the 2 cardboard circles. Tie securely around strands between cardboard circles. Remove cardboards and trim to form body of chicken.

Head: Side (make 2). Starting at center with brown and No. 5 hook, ch 2. *1st rnd:* 8 sc in 2nd ch from hook. *2nd rnd:* * Sc in next 2 sc, 2 sc in next sc. Repeat from * around. *3rd rnd:* Sc in next 2 sc, 2 sc in next sc. Repeat from * around. *4th rnd:* * Sc in next 3 sc, 2 sc in next sc. Repeat from * around. *5th rnd:* * Sc in next 4 sc, 2 sc in next sc. Repeat from * around. *6th to 10th rnds incl:* Sc in each sc around. *11th rnd:* * Sc in next 4 sc, work off 2 sc as 1 sc (1 sc decreased). Repeat from * around. Work in rnds of sc, making decreases where increases were made, until 8 sc remain. Stuff head with scraps of yarn or cotton batting. *Next rnd:* * Work off 2 sc as 1 sc. Repeat from * around. Sew up opening.

Beak: Starting at tip with 2 strands of yellow pearl cotton and No. 1 hook, ch 2. *1st rnd:* 4 sc in 2nd ch from hook. *2nd rnd:* * Sc in next sc, 2 sc in next sc. Repeat from * around. *3rd rnd:* Sc in next sc, 2 sc in next sc. Repeat from * around. Now sc in each sc around until 6 rnds in all have been completed. Break off. Stuff beak and sew in place.

Comb: Starting at base with 2 strands of red pearl cotton, ch 10. *1st row:* Sc in 2nd ch from hook, sc in next ch, half dc in next ch, 2 dc in next ch, 2 tr in next ch, 2 dc in next ch, half dc in next ch, sc in next 2 ch. Ch 1, turn. *2nd row:* Sc in each st across. Break off.

Wattle: With 2 strands of red, ch 2. *1st rnd:* 6 sc in 2nd ch from hook. *2nd and 3rd rnds:* Sc in each sc around. Break off.

Sew comb and wattle in place. Sew a sequin on each side of head for eyes. Sew head in place.

Two-Faced Bunny
(Plate 24)

Materials Needed: 1¾-ounce ball each of baby blue and baby pink Chadwick's Red Heart Baby Wool; plastic crochet hook No. 6.

For key to abbreviations, see page 128.

Use yarn double throughout.

Body and Head: Starting at bottom with blue, ch 12. *1st row:* Sc in 2nd ch from hook, sc in each ch across (11 sc). Ch 1, turn. *2nd row:* 2 sc in first sc, sc in each sc across, ending with 2 sc in last sc (13 sc). Ch 1, turn. *3rd row:* Repeat 2nd row (15 sc). *4th to 14th rows incl:* Sc in each sc across, Ch 1, turn. *15th, 16th, and 17th rows:* Skip first sc (1 sc decreased), sc in each sc across to last 2 sc, skip 1 sc, sc in last sc (another sc decreased—9 sc at end of 17th row). *18th row:* Sc in each sc across. Ch 1, turn. *19th, 20th, and 21st rows:* Inc 1 sc, sc in each sc across, increasing 1 sc in last sc (15 sc at end of 21st row). *22nd row:* Sc in each sc across. Repeat the last row 4 more times. *27th and 28th rows:* Dec 1 sc, sc in each sc across, decreasing the last sc. Ch 1, turn. Break off at end of last row.

With pink make another piece like this. Sew these pieces together, leaving an opening. Stuff firmly and sew up opening.

Ear: Starting at center with blue, ch 12. *1st row:* Sc in 2nd ch from hook and in each ch across, ending with 3 sc in last ch. Working along opposite side of starting chain, make sc in each ch across. Ch 1, turn. *2nd and 3rd rows:* Sc in each sc across, in-

PLATE 24 TWO-FACED BUNNY

creasing 3 sc at rounded end. Ch 1, turn. Break off. Make 2 blue and 2 pink ears. Sew a pink and a blue ear together. Place straight edge of ear to head and sew.

Foot (Make 4—2 pink and 2 blue): Ch 6. *1st row:* Sc in 2nd ch from hook and in each ch across. Ch 1, turn. *2nd and 3rd rows:* Sc in each sc across. Ch 1, turn. Break off at end of 3rd row. Sew pink and blue pieces together, stuff and sew in place.

Paw (Make 4—2 blue and 2 pink): *1st rnd:* Ch 2, 4 sc in 2nd ch from hook. *2nd rnd:* 2 sc in each sc around. *3rd rnd:* Sc in each sc around. *4th rnd:* Dec 4 sc evenly around. Break off. Stuff and sew in place on body.

Tail: Make a pompon with remainder of pink and blue and sew in place.

Face: Embroider with scraps of cotton.

Bashful Bunny
(Plate 25)

This is such a simple, basic pattern that you could adapt it to make other animals from drawings made by your children. They would, of course, especially love those.

Materials Needed: 9″ x 21″ piece of felt, pink or blue; ½ yard ribbon, ½″ wide, to contrast with felt; J. & P. Coats or Clark's O.N.T. Six Strand Embroidery Floss—a few strands each of black, red and tan; J. & P. Coats or Clark's O.N.T. Mercerized Sewing Thread—1 spool to match felt; cotton batting; tracing or tissue paper; dressmaker's carbon paper.

Making the Pattern: You can enlarge the pattern to any size you like. Here it is shown about half the size in which it would usually be made. When you have cut yours (and marked the lines and marks carefully) place it on the felt, as shown in the cutting chart, pin it carefully, and cut out the pieces.

Transferring the Features: Unpin lower part of head pattern and slip a piece of carbon paper, face down, between pattern and felt. With a sharp pencil, go over all lines carefully.

Do this tracing on a hard, flat surface.

Embroidery: Use three strands of embroidery floss throughout. For eyeballs use tan; work in satin stitch. For mouth and nose use red; work in outline stitch. For eyebrows, eyes, and legs use black; work in outline stitch.

For whiskers, use six strands of black floss. Stitch through to wrong side, leaving 1½″ of floss hanging on right side. Secure the whiskers by stitching twice through one of the nose stitches on wrong side. Stitch to right side through mark on opposite side of nose. Leave 1½″ of floss hanging on that side. Repeat for second pair of whiskers. Trim whiskers: upper pair to 1″, lower pair to 1¼″.

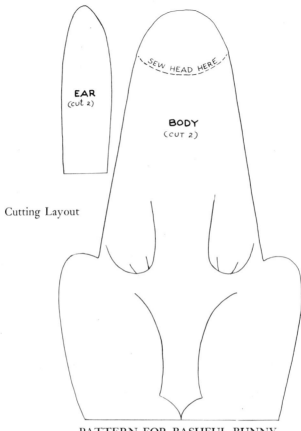

EAR
(cut 2)

SEW HEAD HERE

BODY
(CUT 2)

Cutting Layout

PATTERN FOR BASHFUL BUNNY

Making the Rabbit: 1. Pin the body sections together, matching edges. Baste completely around the body ¼" in from edge, leaving 2" open at top of neck.

2. With matching thread, overcast neatly as shown. Keep the stitches small and close together. Stuff the body with cotton batting. Finish overcasting the opening at the neck.

3. Pin the two head sections together, matching edges. Fold a tuck in each ear, as shown, and insert ¼" of ear between head

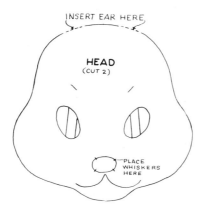

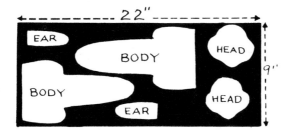

sections at place indicated on pattern. Pin. Starting at chin, baste around head ¼″ from edge.

4. Overcast neatly as before, leaving 2″ open at chin. At ears, put needle through all thicknesses. Stuff head with cotton batting and close opening at chin.

5. Place head in position shown on pattern; pin; baste. Hem chin and back of head to neck. Tie ribbon in a bow around neck.

PLATE 25 BASHFUL BUNNY

Easter Bunny
(Plate 26)

Materials Needed: 2 balls white, 1 ball salmon J. & P. Coats "Knit-Crosheen," Article A 64; scraps of hunter green, pink, black, and yellow; 3 sequins; steel crochet hook No. 7.

For key to abbreviations, see page 128.

Use thread double throughout.

Gauge: 5 sc make 1 inch; 6 rnds make 1 inch.

Body: Starting at bottom with white, ch 2. *1st rnd:* 6 sc in 2nd ch from hook. *2nd rnd:* 2 sc in each sc around. *3rd rnd:* * Sc in next sc, 2 sc in next sc (1 sc increased). Repeat from * around. *4th rnd:* Sc in each sc around, increasing 6 sc evenly around. Repeat 4th rnd until piece measures 1″ from center. Now sc in each sc around until piece measures 3″ from last increase rnd. *Next rnd:* Sc in each sc around, decreasing 6 sc evenly around— to dec 1 sc, work off 2 sc as 1 sc. Repeat the last rnd until all sc are worked off, stuffing firmly before opening becomes too small. Fasten off.

Head: Starting at nose with white, ch 2. *1st rnd:* 4 sc in 2nd ch from hook. *2nd rnd:* 2 sc in each sc around. *3rd rnd:* * Sc in next sc, 2 sc in next sc. Repeat from * around. *4th rnd:* Sc in each sc around, increasing 4 sc evenly around. Repeat 4th rnd until there are 36 sc on rnd. Now sc in each sc around, until piece measures ½″ from last increase rnd. *Next rnd:* Sc in each sc around, decreasing 6 sc evenly around. Repeat the last rnd until all sc are worked off, stuffing firmly before opening becomes too small. Fasten off.

Hind Leg (Make 2): Starting at paw with white, ch 2. *1st rnd:* 6 sc in 2nd ch from hook. *2nd rnd:* 2 sc in each sc around.

3rd rnd: * Sc in next sc, 2 sc in next sc. Repeat from * around. Now sc in each sc around until piece measures 1¼" from last increase rnd. *Next rnd:* 2 sc in each sc around. Now sc in each sc around until piece measures 1" from last increase rnd. *Next rnd:* Sc in each sc around, decreasing 6 sc evenly around. Repeat the last rnd until all sc are worked off, stuffing before opening becomes too small. Fasten off.

Foreleg (Make 2): Work as for hind leg until 3rd rnd has been completed. Now sc in each sc around until piece measures ¾" from last increase rnd. *Next rnd:* 2 sc in each sc around. Complete as for hind leg.

Ear (Make 2): Starting at center with white, ch 14. *1st rnd:* Sc in 2nd ch from hook. Sc in each ch across, 3 sc in last ch. Working along opposite side of starting chain, sc in each ch across, 3 sc in last ch. *2nd and 3rd rnds:* Sc in each sc around, increasing 3 sc at each end. Break off. With one strand of pink, work a row of sc around ear. Break off.

Sew ears in place on head. Sew head and legs in place on body.

Eye (Make 2): With pink ch 2. *1st rnd:* 6 sc in 2nd ch from hook. *2nd rnd:* 2 sc in each sc around. Break off.

Sew eyes in place on head. Sew a sequin in center of each eye and on tip for nose. With black, embroider mouth as illustrated. With 2 strands of pink, work 3 over-and-over sts over the tip of each leg, for paw.

Tail: Cut 2 circles of cardboard, each 1" in diameter. Then cut out a circle ½" in diameter at center of each 1" circle. Place one cardboard circle on top of the other. * Cut 4 strands of white, each about 4 yards long. Draw one end of these strands through center of circle from back, pass them over outer edge and draw them through center of circle again (thus covering cardboard). Continue in this manner until thread is all used up.

PLATE 26 EASTER BUNNY

Repeat from * until center of circle is completely filled in. With sharp scissors or razor cut yarn between the 2 cardboard circles at outer edge. Cut 2 strands of white about 10″ long. Double these strands and slip between the 2 cardboard circles. Tie securely around strands between cardboard circles. Remove cardboards and trim evenly.

Sew tail in place on body.

Basket Base: Starting at base with yellow, ch 9. *1st row:* Sc in 2nd ch from hook; sc in each ch across. Ch 1, turn. *2nd row:* Sc in each sc across. Ch 1, turn. Repeat 2nd row until piece measures 1½″. Break off.

Basket Sides: With yellow, sc closely all around base. Now sc in each sc around until sides measure 1½″. Drop yellow, attach 2 strands of hunter green and sc in each sc around. Break off.

Strap: With hunter green make a chain to measure 5 inches. *1st row:* Sc in 2nd ch from hook, sc in each ch across. Break off.

Sew strap to basket as illustrated.

Carrot: With salmon, work as for hind leg until 2nd rnd has been completed. Now sc in each sc around until piece measures 1″. *Next rnd:* Sc in each sc around, increasing 3 sc evenly around. Repeat the last rnd 2 more times. *Next rnd:* Sc in each sc around, decreasing 6 sc evenly around. Repeat the last rnd until all sc have been worked off, stuffing firmly before opening becomes too small. Fasten off.

Top: With 2 strands of hunter green, make a chain 7″ long. Break off. Loop chain and sew in place at top of carrot, as illustrated.

Sew carrot to right foreleg.

Cuddly Bunny
(Plate 27)

Materials Needed: American Thread Co. "Dawn" knitting worsted, Article W 11, W 15, W 41, W 42 or "Dawn" Paradise yarn, Article W 52: 2 ounces white, 1 ounce pink; 1 ball white "Star" pearl cotton, Article 90, size 5; 3 yards lightweight white hat wire; ½ yard pink ribbon, ½" wide; bone crochet hook No. 2 or No. 3.

For key to abbreviations, see page 128.

Body and Head Pompons: * Over a 3" cardboard wind white wool 23 times, slip from cardboard and tie around center with pearl cotton, cut each end, repeat from * 12 times.

Legs, Arms, and Tail: Over a 2½" cardboard wind 13 white and 9 pink pompons in same manner as body pompons.

Neck: Over a 2" cardboard wind 2 white pompons. Cut wire in 4 pieces (2 pieces 32" and 2 pieces 22") and fold each piece in half.

To Assemble Legs: Place a pink pompon in center of 32" wire, cross wire over center of pompon and tie. Place another pink pompon over center of last pompon, cross wire over, and tie. Then * place white pompon over center of last pompon, cross wire and tie. Repeat from * twice. Work another leg in same manner. Place the 2 legs together and tie the 4 wires tight to hold legs firmly. Separate the wires, having 2 wires on each side.

To Assemble Body: * Place a body pompon in center of the 2 wires, cross wires over center of pompon and twist wires. Repeat from * 6 times. Tie all wires after last pompon.

PLATE 27   CUDDLY BUNNY

Arms: Using the 22″ wire, work arms in same manner as legs, using 2 pink and 3 white for each arm. Tie each arm wire to 2 of the body wires, then tie all 8 wires firmly, cut 4 of the shorter wires, leaving 4 to work neck and head. Tie the 2 neck pompons, then tie the remaining 6 pompons in the same manner for head. Tie wires firmly at top. Thread each wire in needle and draw down through the head. Cut ends. Trim body, legs, arms, neck and head. Tie the 2 tail pompons with thread and sew in position.

Ears: With pink, ch 7, 6 sc on ch, ch 1 to turn each row. *2nd row:* 1 sc in each sc. *3rd and 4th rows:* Increase 1 sc at beginning of each row. *5th and 6th rows:* 1 sc in each sc. Repeat the last 4 rows twice. *15th row:* Decrease 1 sc at beginning of row. Repeat 15th row 9 times, then work 1 row of sc all around ear, working 1 sc in each row and 1 sc in each sc.

Break yarn and work another ear in same manner.

Eye: Ch 2, 6 sc in 1st st of ch, join, and break yarn. Work another eye in same manner.

Sew ears in position at back of head, sew eyes in, and tie 2 strands of yarn in for whiskers. Place ribbon around neck and tie in bow.

Easter-Parade Poodles
(Plate 28)

Materials Needed: American Thread Co. "Dawn" black and gray sock and sweater yarn: 2 ounces will make 1 large poodle—1 ounce will make 2 small poodles; 1 skein black "star" six strand embroidery cotton, Article 50; steel crochet hook No. 6; 25″ length of heavy wire; 18″ length of heavy wire; 2 10″ lengths of heavy wire; gray crepe paper for large poodle; 3 pipe cleaners for small poodle; 2 yards of fine wire.

For key to abbreviations, see page 128.

PLATE 28 EASTER-PARADE POODLES

Large Poodle

Bend heavy wire as illustrated in Figs. A-B-C-D-E and twist fine wire tightly where top of legs and body meet, as in Fig. F.

Cut gray paper in 1″ bias strips. Wrap around each leg until they are 1″ in circumference. Wrap head, then neck until it is 2″ in circumference and body until it is 3″ in circumference.

Feet: With embroidery cotton ch 2, 6 sc in 2nd st from hook. Do not join or turn this or following rnds. Place a marker at beginning of each rnd. *Next 4 rnds:* 1 sc in each sc, join last rnd, cut thread, leaving a length for sewing. Place a foot on each leg and sew to leg.

Nose and Head Sections: With black, ch 4, dc in 4th st from hook, 8 dc in same space. Join, but do not turn. *2nd rnd:* Ch 3, 1 dc in each of the next 9 sts, join, cut thread. *3rd rnd:* Attach gray, ch 3, 1 dc in each st, join. *4th rnd:* Ch 3, dc in next dc, * 1 dc in next dc, 2 dc in next dc. Repeat from * all around. Join. *Next 2 rnds:* Working in dc, increase 7 sts evenly spaced, ch 3 at end of last rnd and turn. *Next 3 rows:* 1 dc in each st, ch 3 to turn all rows, cut yarn, leaving a length. If necessary place a little cotton in nose. Place section on head, having opening at neck edge.

Sew last row together.

With gray wind entire body tightly, keeping yarn very close together and leaving about ¼″ of each foot free.

Small Pompons for Head: Wind gray over a 1″ cardboard 100 times. Tie one end, using 3 strands of yarn. Cut opposite end and comb (all pompons are worked in same manner). Work 2 more pompons. Place one on each side of head and sew in position through crepe paper. Tie ends together.

Ears: Wind gray over an 8″ cardboard 18 times, cut both

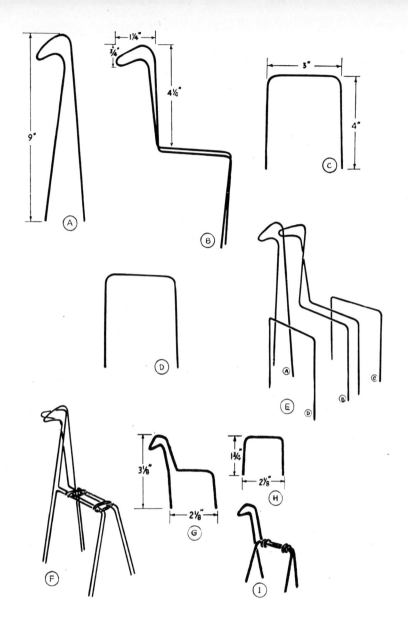

EASTER-PARADE POODLES – STEP-BY-STEP

ends, and tie one end. Divide into 3 sections and braid loosely. Tie other end. Trim and comb ends. Place on top of head and sew at center.

Large Pompon for Head: Wind gray 180 times over a 1¾" cardboard. Sew to top of head on top of braided ears. Sew remaining small pompon at back of neck below large pompon.

Pompons for Lower End of Neck and Front Legs: Wind gray 150 times over a 1½" cardboard. Make 3 more pompons in same manner. Make 2 smaller pompons (100 times over a 1" cardboard).

Tie one large pompon where neck joins body and another in front of neck. Tie a small pompon on each side between these, a little lower down. Tie a large pompon where each leg joins body section.

Make 4 more pompons (60 times over a ⅝" cardboard). Tie 2 on each leg about 1" from foot.

Pompons for Tail and Hind Legs: Make 3 pompons (150 times over a 1½" cardboard). Tie one on each hind leg where leg meets body, and tie one on body for tail. Make 4 pompons (60 times over a ⅝" cardboard). Tie 2 on each leg about 1" from foot. Trim and shape poodle as illustrated. With black, embroider eyes, as illustrated. Tie with bows if desired.

Small Poodle

Join 2 pipe cleaners together and bend as illustrated in Fig. G. Bend another pipe cleaner as illustrated in Fig. H. Twist fine wire tightly where top of legs and body meet, as in Fig. I.

With black, wind entire body very tightly, starting at top of leg and working downward to about 1/16" from end, then winding upward. Wind black 9 times over center part of body and 5 times over neck. Wind enough black over head to cover entire section. With embroidery cotton, embroider nose and eyes in satin stitch.

Small Pompons for Head: Wind black 40 times over a ⅜" cardboard. Sew to one side of head. Work 2 more pompons in same manner. Sew one on opposite side of head and the other at back of head.

Ears: Cut 6 strands of yarn 6" long. Divide in 3 sections and braid loosely. Tie each end. Trim and comb ends. Place on top of head and sew at center.

Large Pompon for Head: Wind black 80 times over a ½" cardboard. Sew to top of head on top of braided ears.

Pompons for Front Legs: Wind black 40 times over a ⅜" cardboard. Tie pompon to top of leg where leg meets body. Make 3 more pompons in same manner. Tie one to other leg and remaining pompons to top of body at lower end of neck, at joinings.

Pompons for Hind Legs: Wind black 40 times over a ⅜" cardboard. Tie to top of legs where leg meets body. Make one more pompon in same manner. Sew to top of opposite leg.

Pompon for Tail: Wind black 80 times over a ½" cardboard. Tie to body.

Pompons for Lower Part of Legs: Wind black 20 times over a ¼" cardboard. Tie to front of leg about ½" from end. Make another pompon in same manner. Tie in back of leg. Finish other legs in same manner. Trim and shape poodle as illustrated. Tie with bows if desired.

Dolly Dress
(Plate 29)

Materials Needed: 2 balls desired color, 1 ball white of either: American Thread Co. "Puritan" crochet cotton, Article 40; or "De Luxe" crochet cotton, Article 346; or "Star" crochet cotton, Article 20, size 30; "Star" six strand embroidery cotton, Article 50, assorted colors; 1½ yards narrow white ribbon. If doll is 10″, use one of first two crochet cottons with steel No. 7 needle. If doll is 7″ or 8″, use "Star" crochet cotton with steel No. 11 needle. 1½ yards narrow white ribbon.

For key to abbreviations, see page 128.

Skirt of Dress: With color, ch 46, 2 dc in 4th st from hook, 3 dc in each remaining st of ch, ch 3, turn. *2nd row:* Working in back loop of sts, dc in same space, 2 dc in each remaining dc, join. *3rd rnd:* Working in back loop of sts for remainder of skirt, ch 1 and work 1 sc in each dc, join each round. *4th and 5th rnds:* Ch 1, 1 sc in each sc. *6th rnd:* Ch 3, 1 dc in each sc. *7th, 8th, and 9th rnds:* Ch 1 and work 1 sc in each st. Repeat the last 4 rnds 4 times. *26th rnd:* * Ch 5, skip 2 sts, sc in next st,

repeat from * all around ending round with ch 2, dc in same
space as beginning (this brings thread in position for next round).
27th rnd: * Ch 5, sc in next loop, repeat from * all around ending
rnd with ch 2, dc in dc. *28th rnd:* Same as last round but ending
round with ch 5, sc in dc. *29th rnd:* * 3 sc in next loop, repeat
from * all around, join, cut thread.

Bodice: With right side of skirt toward you, attach thread in
1st st at top of skirt, ch 3 and work 1 dc in each st of starting ch,
ch 1 (44 dc counting the ch 3 as 1 dc), turn. *2nd row:* Working
in front loop of sts, work 1 sc in each dc, ch 1, turn. *3rd row:*
Working in back loop of sts, work * 1 sc in each of the next 5
sts, 2 sc in next st, repeat from * across row to within the last 8
sts, 1 sc in each of the last 8 sts, ch 1, turn.

Work all even-numbered rows in front loop of sts and odd-
numbered rows in back loop of sts for remainder of bodice.

4th row: 1 sc in each sc (50 sc), ch 3, turn. *5th row:* * 1 dc
in each of the next 4 sc, 2 dc in next sc, repeat from * across row
to within the last 9 sts, 1 dc in each remaining st, ch 1, turn. *6th
row:* Working in sc, increase 1 sc in every 4th st, ch 1, turn
(72 sc), then work 2 rows even in sc, ch 3 to turn last row. *9th
row:* 1 dc in each st, ch 1, turn. Work 3 rows even in sc, ch 3 to
turn last row. *13th row:* 1 dc in each of the next 11 sts, ch 10,
skip 9 sts, 1 dc in each of the next 30 sts, ch 10, skip 9 sts, 1 dc
in each of the last 12 sts, ch 1, turn. *14th row:* 1 sc in each dc
and 1 sc in each st of ch, ch 1, turn. *15th row:* ** 1 sc in each of
the next 5 sc, decrease in next 2 sts (to decrease: * insert hook in
next st, pull loop through, repeat from * once, thread over and
pull through all loops at one time), repeat from ** across row
ending row with 1 sc in each of the last 4 sc, ch 1, turn. *16th row:*
Working in sc, decrease every 9th st, ch 1, turn, then work 1
row even, ch 1, turn. *18th row:* Repeat the 16th row. *19th row:*

1 sc in each of the next 12 sc, * decrease in next 2 sts, 1 sc in each of the next 5 sts, repeat from * 3 times, decrease in next 2 sts, 1 sc in each remaining st, without cutting thread, work a row of sc around back opening working a ch 3 loop at neck, center of bodice and waistline on each side for ribbon loops, cut thread.

Collar: With wrong side toward you, attach thread in 1st free loop of st of 18th row, working on right side, * ch 3, skip 1 st, sc in free loop of next st, repeat from * across neck, ch 3, turn. *2nd row:* Sc in next loop, * ch 3, sc in next loop, repeat from * to end of row, ch 1, turn. *3rd row:* * 3 sc in next loop, repeat from * across row, cut thread.

Sleeve: Attach thread in 1st st of ch 10 at top of armhole, sc in same space, 1 sc in each of the next 9 sts of ch, ch 3, turn. *2nd row:* Sc in next sc, * ch 3, sc in next sc, repeat from * 7 times, ch 3, turn. *3rd row:* Sc in 1st loop, * ch 3, sc in next loop, sl st in base of next row at side of armhole, ch 1, turn. *4th row:* 3 sc in each loop, sl st in base of next row at side of armhole, cut thread. Work other sleeve in same manner.

Place dress on doll and tie with 3 small ribbon bows in back, inserting ribbon through the loops.

Pantalettes: With color, ch 49, trc in 5th st from hook, 1 trc in each remaining st of ch, turn. *2nd row:* Ch 4 (counts as 1 trc), working in back loop of sts only, 1 trc in each of the next 4 trc, 2 trc in next trc, * 1 trc in each of the next 5 trc, 2 trc in next trc, repeat from * across row, ending row with 1 trc in each of the last 4 sts. *3rd row:* Working in front loop of sts, work, same as 2nd row, but ending row with 1 trc in each of the last 5 sts. *4th row:* Ch 4, turn, working in trc and back loop of sts, increase 7 trc evenly spaced, join in 4th st of ch (68 trc), cut thread, turn.

Work all even-numbered rows in back loop of sts and all odd-numbered rows in front loop of sts for remainder of pantalettes.

5th row: Start leg. Attach thread in 18th st from joining, ch 4, 1 trc in each of the next 33 trc, join in 4th st of ch, ch 4, turn. *6th row:* 1 trc in each trc, join in 4th st of ch, ch 4, turn. Repeat the last row 8 times or length desired, turn. *15th row:* Ch 1 and work 1 sc in each trc, join, cut thread.

Ruffle: Attach thread in 1st free loop of st of 14th row, ch 3, dc in same space, * 2 dc in free loop of next st, repeat from * all around, join. *2nd row:* Ch 1 and working in back loop of sts, work 1 sc in each dc, join, cut thread.

Work a ruffle in free loop of sts of 13th, 12th, and 11th rows in same manner.

Finish other leg in same manner.

Apron and Band: With white, ch 46, trc in 5th st from hook, 1 trc in each remaining st of ch, cut thread. *2nd row:* Attach white in 13th st from end and working in back loop of sts, ch 4, 2 trc in same space with ch, * 3 trc in next trc, repeat from * to within the last 12 trc, ch 5, turn. *3rd row:* Working through both loops, skip 1 trc, trc in next trc, * ch 1, skip 1 trc, trc in next trc, repeat from * across row ending row with ch 1, skip 1 trc, trc in 4th st of ch, ch 4, turn. *4th row:* 1 trc in each mesh and 1 trc in each trc working last trc in 4th st of end ch, ch 5, turn. Repeat the last 2 rows twice but ch 1 at end of last row. Work a row of sc up side of apron, around entire band, down opposite side of apron and across lower edge. Cut thread.

Bib: Attach thread in 15th st of band, ch 4 (counts as 1 trc), 1 trc in each of the next 15 sts, ch 4, turn. Work 2 rows even in trc. *4th row:* Ch 1, turn, 1 sc in each of the 1st 3 trc for strap, ch 1, turn. *Next row:* 1 sc in each sc, ch 1, turn. Repeat the last row 31 times, ch 4, turn, 1 trc in each of the next 2 sc, cut thread.

Attach thread at opposite side and work another strap in same manner, cut thread. Attach thread at waist band and work a row of sc around entire bib and straps, cut thread.

Lace ribbon through band, then lace through each end of strap and tie in back.

Snood: With white, ch 36, sc in 6th st from hook, * ch 5, skip 1 st of ch, sc in next st, repeat from * across ch, ch 5, turn. *2nd row:* Sc in next loop, * ch 5, sc in next loop, repeat from * across row, ch 4, turn. *3rd, 4th, and 5th rows:* Sc in next loop, * ch 4, sc in next loop, repeat from * to end of row, ch 4, turn. *6th row:* Sc in next loop, * ch 4, sc in next loop, repeat from * to within the last 2 loops, ch 4, sc in next loop, sc in next loop, ch 4, turn. Repeat the last row 6 times. *13th row:* Sc in next loop, * ch 4, sc in next loop, repeat from * across row working 2 sc in last loop, then work 2 sc in each loop around entire snood, join, cut thread. This end is top of snood.

Lace ribbon through sides and lower edge and tie in position on head.

Bulletin Boards

Every well-equipped home should have at least one bulletin board, and I think the happiest arrangement of all is to have one for each person in the house—in his own room, on the wall outside his room, or wherever is preferred. A simple bulletin board is quite easy to make, especially if the man of the house is handy with tools. The best possible surface is cork, but there are other porous materials that are quite satisfactory. For Easter you might make a seasonable, special-purpose board out of cardboard. Decorate it with birds and flowers and then in the center

BUNNY RABBIT SUIT

of the board list all the signs of spring to watch for—the first robin, the first crocus, or whatever is indigenous to your part of the country. Present it to a youngster with a box of stars. Tell him to paste a star beside each sign of spring as he discovers it.

Bunny-Rabbit Suit

The most appropriate costume, if your small child has or is invited to a fancy-dress party at Easter time, is a bunny-rabbit suit. You will, of course, need a pattern for this, and research leads me to believe that the best one to be found and the easiest to make is McCall's Pattern 1485. The sketch shows what the suit looks like when finished.

12

Gifts to Make for Grown-Ups

Easter has become as important a time for giving gifts to those we love as Christmas or a birthday. During the long Lenten evenings, and perhaps afternoons too, when social activity is at a minimum, you can occupy yourself happily with the making of Easter presents.

For the Ladies

There are many lovely things to make for girl and women friends, and here are a few suggestions, just to set your mind working!

Scarves

At the moment, scarves of all kinds are exceedingly fashionable. They may be any size at all—no bigger than a large handkerchief or almost as big as a stole. The materials available are enough to set anyone off into a happy flurry of scarf-making that lasts all of Lent! Beautiful Liberty silks, for instance, have again become quite widely available. A small scarf of Liberty silk twisted through a string of pearls, to wear with a round-necked sweater, is something any smart woman would love. Just roll the edge—and there you are. There are also wonderful cottons from which scarves can be made. For young girls, large, square scarves which they can wear as kerchiefs on their heads are most popular. These are presents which can be used and enjoyed all spring and summer.

Sachets

It is always fun to give people things you know they would like but would never spend the time or money to make or buy for themselves. Sachets are that sort of present. Any woman's bureau drawers are more delightful—and their contents stay that way when worn—if they are equipped with pleasantly scented sachets. It's thoughtful, if you can, to discover whether the person to whom you plan to give such a present has a single perfume which is her favorite. If you can't, a spicy scent is usually a safer bet than a very heavy or very sweet one. Give, perhaps, three sachets in varying sizes, each enclosed in a different pastel shade of silk and tied with either matching or contrasting ribbon. They are beautiful, easy to make, and inexpensive gifts.

Miscellaneous

Hat pins covered with material to match (and thus disappear into the background) or contrast with an Easter bonnet are delightful gifts—and so easy to make. Just buy good strong pins about 3″ long, with fair-sized heads and cover them with whatever you like, being careful to sew the end of the cover which you slip over the head of the pin tightly enough so that it can't fall off.

Corsages made of silk or felt are especially fun for little girls. And of course, if you are an expert seamstress, there's something particularly Eastery about lovely handmade lingerie or blouses as gifts.

Stoles

Stoles have become very popular with smart women in recent years. They may be made of any material at all and sewn, knitted, or crocheted. With the coming summer in mind, a stole made of a heavy cotton or cotton-and-rayon-blend sharkskin, edged with a sturdy cotton lace is a most useful thing to own. Velvet ones are wonderful for cool summer evenings, as are those knitted of thin wool. Any of these can be made in either rectangular or triangular shape. And any lady from eighteen (or under) to eighty (or older) will adore the stole you make her for Easter— whatever kind it may be.

Tatted Handkerchief
(Plate 30)

Materials Needed: 5 60-yard balls white American Thread Company "Star" mercerized tatting cotton, Article 25; 1 shuttle and 1 ball; 4½″ square of fine, thin linen.

PLATE 30

TATTED

HANDKERCHIEF

For key to abbreviations, see page 128.

Make a very narrow hem all around the square of linen.

1st row: With shuttle only, r, 3 d, 3 p sep by 3 d, 3 d, cl r. ⅛" space. ** Work a clover leaf at corner as follows: 3 d, join to last p of last r, 3 d, 2 p sep by 3 d, 3 d, cl r. LR, 3 d, join to last p of last r, 3 d, 3 p sep by 1 d, 3 d, p, 3 d, cl r. R, 3 d, join to last p of previous r, 3 d, 2 p sep by 3 d, 3 d, cl r. * ⅛" space. R, 3 d, join to last p of previous r, 3 d, 2 p sep by 3 d, 3 d, cl r. Repeat from * 20 times. Repeat from ** all around, having 21 rings on each side between corners. Sew this 1st row to square of linen. *2nd row:* R, 3 d, p, 3 d, join to p of 1st r of clover leaf at corner, 3 d, p, 3 d, cl r. ⅛" space, turn. R, 3 d, 5 p sep by 2 d, 3 d, cl r, turn. Leave a ⅛" space between all rings in this row. R, 3 d, join to p of 1st r made 3 d, join to 1st p of large r of clover of 1st row, 3 d, p, 3 d, cl r, turn. R, 3 d, join to p of opposite r, 3 d, p, 3 d, p, 3 d, cl r. LR, 3 d, join to last p of last r, 2 d, 4 p sep by 2 d, 3 d, cl r. R, 3 d, join to last p of last r, 3 d, p, 3 d, p, 3 d, cl r, turn. R, 3 d, join to p of opposite r, 3 d, join to next p of large r of clover, 3 d, p, 3 d, cl r, turn. R, 3 d, join to last p of opposite r, 2 d, 4 p sep by 2 d, 3 d, cl r, turn. R, 3 d, join to p of opposite r, 3 d, join to p of 3rd r of clover leaf, 3 d, p, 3 d, cl r, turn. * R, 3 d, join to last p of opposite r, 2 d, 4 p sep by 2 d, 3 d, cl r, turn. R, 3 d, join to last p of opposite r, 3 d, join to p of next r of 1st row, 3 d, p, 3 d, cl r, turn. Repeat from * across each side and work other corners to correspond.

3rd row: With shuttle and ball, R, 4 d, 3 p sep by 4 d, 4 d, cl r.
LR, 4 d, join to last p of last r, 4 d, 3 p sep by 2 d, 4 d, p, 4 d,
cl r. R, 4 d, join to last p of last r, 4 d, 2 p sep by 4 d, 4 d, cl r,
turn. Ch, 5 d, 2 p sep by 2 d, 2 d, join to 1st free p of center r of
clover of 2nd row, 5 d, turn. R, 4 d, p, 4 d, join to center p of
last r made, 4 d, p, 4 d, cl r. LR, 4 d, join to last p of last r, 4 d,
7 p sep by 1 d, 4 d, p, 4 d, cl r. R, 4 d, join to last p of last r,
4 d, p, 4 d, p, 4 d, cl r, turn. Ch, 5 d, skip 1 p, join to next p of
corner of r of 2nd row, 2 d, 2 p sep by 2 d, 5 d, turn. R, 4 d, p,
4 d, join to center p of last r, 4 d, p, 4 d, cl r. LR, 4 d, join to
last p of last r, 4 d, 3 p sep by 2 d, 4 d, cl r. R, 4 d, join to last
p of last r, 4 d, p, 4 d, p, 4 d, cl r, turn. Ch 5 d, 2 p sep by 2 d,
2 d, skip last row of clover, join to center p of next r of 2nd row,
2 d, 2 p sep by 2 d, 5 d, turn. * Work another clover leaf joining to last clover leaf in same manner, turn. Ch, 5 d, 2 p sep by
2 d, 2 d, skip 1 r of 2nd row, join to center p of next r of 2nd
row, 2 d, 2 p sep by 2 d, 5 d, turn. Repeat from * across sides
and work corners same as 1st corner. *4th row:* R, 4 d, 3 p, sep
by 4 d, 4 d, cl r. LR, 4 d, join to last p of last r, 4 d, 3 p, sep by
1 d, 1 d, join to 2nd free p of large r at corner of 3rd row, 1 d,
3 p sep by 1 d, 4 d, p, 4 d, cl r. R, 4 d, join to last p of last r, 4 d,
2 p sep by 4 d, 4 d, cl r, turn. Ch, 6 d, 6 p sep by 1 d, 6 d, turn.
R, 4 d, p, 4 d, join to center p of last r, 4 d, p, 4 d, cl r. LR, 4 d
join to last p of last r, 4 d, join to last free p of last large r, 1 d,
4 p sep by 1 d, 4 d, p, 4 d, cl r. R, 4 d, join to last p of last r,
4 d, p, 4 d, p, 4 d, cl r, turn. Ch, 5 d, 12 p sep by 1 d, 5 d, turn.
R, 4 d, p, 4 d, join to center p of last r, 4 d, p, 4 d, cl r. LR, 4 d,
join to last p of last r, 4 d, join to last p of last large r, 1 d, 4 p sep
by 1 d, 4 d, p, 4 d, cl r. R, 4 d, join to last p of last r, 4 d, p, 4 d, p,
4 d, cl r, turn. Ch, 6 d, 6 p sep by 1 d, 6 d, turn. R, 4 d, p, 4 d,
join to center p of last r, 4 d, p, 4 d, cl r. LR, 4 d, join to last p

of last r, 4 d, join to last p of last large r, 1 d, 2 p sep by 1 d, 1 d, join to 4th free p of corner r of 3rd row, 1 d, 3 p sep by 1 d, 4 d, p, 4 d, cl r. R, 4 d, join to last p of last r, 4 d, p, 4 d, p, 4 d, cl r, turn. * Ch, 6 d, 6 p sep by 1 d, 6 d turn. R, 4 d, p, 4 d, join to center p of last r, 4 d, p, 4 d, cl r. LR, 4 d, join to last p of last r, 4 d, p, 2 d, join to center p of center r of next clover of 3rd row, 2 d, p, 4 d, p, 4 d, cl r. R, 4 d, join to last p of last r, 4 d, 2 p sep by 4 d, 4 d, cl r, turn. Repeat from * across side, work all corners in same manner. *5th row:* R, 4 d, 3 p sep by 4 d, 4 d, cl r. LR, 4 d, join to last p of last r, 4 d, 3 p sep by 2 d, 4 d, p, 4 d, cl r. R, 4 d, join to last p of last r, 4 d, p, 4 d, p, 4 d, cl r. Ch, 6 d, 2 p sep by 1 d, 1 d, join to 3rd p of 1st ch at corner of 4th row, 1 d, join to next p of same ch, 1 d, 2 p sep by 1 d, 6 d, turn. R, 4 d, p, 4 d, join to center p of last r, 4 d, p, 4 d, cl r. LR, 4 d, join to last p of last r, 4 d, 3 p sep by 2 d, 4 d, p, 4 d, cl r. R, 4 d, join to last p of last r, 4 d, 2 p sep by 4 d, 4 d, cl r. All clovers in this row are made in same manner, turn. Ch, 6 d, 2 p sep by 1 d, 1 d, skip 2 p of corner ch of 4th row, join in next p, 1 d, 2 p sep by 1 d, 6 d, turn. Work another clover, turn. Ch 6 d, 2 p sep by 1 d, 1 d, skip 2 p of same ch of 4th row, join to next p, 1 d, 2 p sep by 1 d, 6 d, turn. Work another clover, turn. Ch, 6 d, 2 p sep by 1 d, 1 d, join to next p of same ch of 4th row, 1 d, 2 p sep by 1 d, 6 d, turn. Work another clover, turn. Ch, 6 d, 2 p sep by 1 d, 1 d, skip 2 p of same ch of 4th row, join in next p, 1 d, 2 p sep by 1 d, 6 d, turn. * Work another clover, turn. Ch, 6 d, 2 p sep by 1 d, 1 d, join to 3rd p of next ch of 4th row, 1 d, join to next p of same ch, 1 d, 2 p sep by 1 d, 6 d, turn. Repeat from * across sides and work all corners in same manner. *6th row:* R, 4 d, 3 p sep by 4 d, 4 d, cl r. LR, 4 d, join to last p of last r, 4 d, p, 2 d, join to center p of corner clover of 5th row, 4 d, p, 4 d, cl r. R, 4 d, join to last p of last r, 4 d, 2 p sep by 4 d, 4 d, cl r, turn.

Ch, 6 d, 8 p sep by 1 d, 6 d, turn. R, 4 d, p, 4 d, join to center p of last r, 4 d, p, 4 d, cl r. LR, 4 d, join to last p of last r, 4 d, join to same center p of corner clover of 5th row, 2 d, p, 4 d, p, 4 d, cl r. R, 4 d, join to last p of last r, 4 d, 2 p sep by 4 d, 4 d, cl r, turn. * Ch, 6 d, 6 p sep by 1 d, 6 d, turn. R, 4 d, p, 4 d, join to center p of last r, 4 d, p, 4 d, cl r. LR, 4 d, join to last p of last r, 4 d, p, 2 d, join to center p of next clover of 5th row, 2 d, p, 4 d, p, 4 d, cl r. R, 4 d, join to last p of last r, 4 d, 4 d, 2 p sep by 4 d, 4 d, cl r, turn. Repeat from * across side and work all corners in same manner. *7th row:* R, 4 d, 3 p sep by 4 d, 4 d, cl r. LR, 4 d, joint to last p of last r, 2 d, 6 p sep by 2 d, 4 d, cl r. R, 4 d, join to last p of last r, 4 d, 2 p sep by 4 d, 4 d, cl r, turn. Ch, 6 d, 2 p sep by 1 d, join to 2nd p of corner ch of 6th row, 1 d, join to next p of same ch, 1 d, 2 p sep by 1 d, 6 d, p, 6 d, turn. R, 3 d, join to center p of last r, 3 d, p, 3 d, cl r, turn. Ch, 4 d, turn. R, 4 d, join to last p of last r, 2 d, 4 p sep by 2 d, 4 d, cl r. R, 4 d, join to last p of last r, 2 d, 6 p sep by 2 d, 4 d, cl r. R, 4 d, join to last p of last r, 2 d, 4 p sep by 2 d, 4 d, cl r, turn. Ch, 4 d, turn. R, 4 d, join to last p of last r, 4 d, p, 4 d, cl r, turn. Ch, 6 d, join to last p of opposite ch, 6 d, 2 p sep by 1 d, skip 2 p of corner ch of 6th row, join to next p, 1 d, join to next p of same ch, 1 d, 2 p sep by 1 d, 6 d, turn. * R, 4 d, p, 4 d, join to last p of last r, 4 d, p, 4 d, cl r. R, 4 d, join to last p of last r, 2 d, 6 p sep by 2 d, 4 d, cl r. R, 4 d, join to last p of last r, 4 d, 2 p sep by 4 d, 4 d, cl r, turn. Ch 6 d, 2 p sep by 1 d, 1 d, join to 3rd p of next ch of 6th row, 1 d, join to next p of same ch, 1 d, 2 p sep by 1 d, 6 d, turn. Repeat from * across side and work all corners in same manner.

Table Scarves

(Plate 31)

Materials Needed: 16 250-yard balls American Thread Company "Star" 6-cord mercerized crochet cotton, Article 77, white; "Star" mercerized crochet cotton, Article 30, size 30, white; steel crochet hooks #11 and #12.

The "ingredients" above will make 2 scarves measuring about 14½" x 63".

For key to abbreviations, see page 128.

With the 6-cord crochet cotton and #11 hook, ch 223, sc in 3rd st from hook for picot, skip 9 sts of ch, sc in next st of ch, * ch 4, sc in 3rd st from hook for picot, ch 4, sc in 3rd st from hook for picot, ch 1, skip 4 sts of ch, sc in next st, repeat from * 41 times, turn. *2nd row:* Ch 9, sc in 3rd st from hook for picot, ch 1, sc between picots of next loop. * ch 4, sc in 3rd st from hook for picot, ch 4, sc in 3rd st from hook for picot, ch 1, (double picot loop), sc between picots of next loop, repeat from * across row, ending with double picot loop, sc in 1st st after last picot of end loop, turn.

Repeat 2nd row until scarf measures about 63 inches, ch 9, turn. *Next row:* Sc between picots of 1st loop. * ch 5, sc between picots of next loop, repeat from * across row.

Edge: Work 5 sc over each loop at each end, and 6 sc over each loop on long sides, 11 sc in corner over ch 9.

Rose: With "Star" crochet cotton and #12 hook, ch 5, join to form a ring, ch 6, dc in ring. * ch 3, dc in ring, repeat from * 3 times, ch 3, join in 3rd st of ch 6. *2nd row:* Over each loop, work 1 sc, 1 sdc, 3 dc, 1 sdc, 1 sc (sdc: thread over, insert in st, pull through and work off all loops at one time). *3rd row:* * Ch 5, sc in back of work between the sc of next 2 petals, repeat from

PLATE 31 TABLE SCARVES

* all round. *4th row:* Over each loop work 1 sc, 1 sdc, 5 dc, 1 sdc, 1 sc. *5th row:* * Ch 7, sc in back of work between next 2 petals, repeat from * all around. *6th row:* Over each loop, work 1 sc, 1 sdc, 7 dc, 1 sdc, 1 sc, sl st in 1st sc, break thread. Work 29 more roses.

Leaf: Ch 13, sc in 2nd st from hook, 1 sc in each of the next 10 sts of ch, 3 sc in next st of ch, working on other side of ch, work 1 sc in each of the next 8 sts, ch 3, turn, picking up the back loop of st throughout. 1 sc in each of the next 9 sc, 3 sc in next sc, 1 sc in each of the next 7 sc, ch 3, turn. * 1 sc in each of the next 8 sc, 3 sc in next sc. 1 sc in each of the next 7 sts, ch 3, turn, repeat from * 5 times, sl st in each of the next 2 sc, break thread. Work 81 more leaves.

Appliqué roses and leaves as illustrated. Work second scarf in the same manner.

Shoulder Bag
(Plate 32)

Materials Needed: 6 balls American Thread Company "Puritan" crochet cotton, Article 40 or "De Luxe" quality crochet cotton, Article 346 (in white or desired color); ½ yard buckram; ½ yard lining; 1 yard grosgrain ribbon 1″ wide; a pair #1 knitting needles; #1 double-pointed needle.

For key to abbreviations, see page 128.

Work bag with a double strand of thread throughout.

Front Section: Cast on 96 sts.

1st row: K 2, p 2, * k 4, p 8, k 4, p 2, repeat from * across row, ending with k 2. *2nd row:* P 2, k 2, * p 4 (purl gore), k 8, p 4 (purl gore), k 2, repeat from * across row ending with p 2. *3rd, 5th, 7th, and 9th rows:* Same as 1st row. *4th, 6th, and 8th*

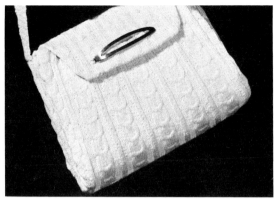

rows: Same as 2nd row. *10th row:* P 2, k 2, * p 4, slip the next 2 sts on a double-pointed needle and hold in back of work, k next 2 sts, then k the 2 sts from double-pointed needle, slip the next 2 sts on a double-pointed needle and hold in front of work, k next 2 sts, then k 2 sts from double-pointed needle, p 4, k 2, repeat from * across row ending with p 2.

Repeat these 10 rows for pattern. Work in pattern until there are 4 cable twists completed.

Next row: Dec 1 st on each side in first and last purl gores leaving only 3 sts in these gores. Work next 9 rows even in pattern.

Next row: K 2, p 2, k 3, p 8, k 1, k 2 tog (decrease), k 1, p 2, k 1, k 2 tog, k 1, * p 8, k 4, p 2, k 4, repeat from * once, p 8, k 1, k 2 tog, k 1, p 2, k 1, k 2 tog, k 1, p 8, k 3, p 2, k 2. Work next 9 rows even in pattern having only 3 purl sts on the decreasing purl gores.

Next row: Dec 1 st in each of the 4 center purl gores, which leaves 3 sts in each purl gore across row, then continue in pattern until piece measures 11″, bind off.

Back Section: Work in same manner as front section until piece measures 11″, then start flap. Decrease 1 st at beginning and end of every 4th row 9 times. Work 2 rows even in pattern. If buttonhole is desired, work next 2 rows as follows: *Next row:* Work even in pattern to center cable, bind off next 8 sts for buttonhole, work remainder of row in pattern. *Next row:* Dec 1 st at beginning and end of row and cast on 8 sts over the bound off sts for buttonhole.

If buttonhole is omitted, work the 2 rows in pattern, decreasing 1 st at beginning and end of 2nd row.

Next 3 rows: Work even in pattern. *Next row:* Dec 1 st at beginning and end of row.

Next 3 rows: Work even in pattern.

Next 7 rows: Dec 1 st at beginning and end of each row.

Next row: Bind off remaining 50 sts.

Gusset: Cast on 24 sts and work in pattern same as on bag, increasing 1 st at beginning and end of each row until there are 52 sts on needle. Work even in pattern until 9 cable twists are completed. Bind off on 2nd row of pattern. Work another gusset in same manner.

Finishing: Block each section. Cut buckram ¼″ smaller than sections. Cut lining same size as bag sections. Sew front and back section of bag together. Sew gussets in position. Sew buckram sections together and insert in bag. Baste knitted section over buckram to hold in position. Sew lining together in same manner as buckram. Place in bag, turn under raw edges and sew to knitted section. Sew 2 plaits on each gusset section. Finish buttonhole and sew button in position.

Shoulder Strap: Cast on 8 sts, and work as follows: *1st and 2nd rows:* * K 2, P 2, repeat from * across each row. *3rd and 4th rows:* * P 2, K 2, repeat from * across each row.

Repeat these 4 rows until strap measures 30″, bind off. Face with ribbon and sew to bag as illustrated.

Plant and Pot Holders
(Plate 33)

Materials Needed: 1 ball color and 1 ball white of American Thread Company "Puritan" crochet cotton Article 40 or "De Luxe" crochet cotton Article 346 *or* 3 balls color and 1 ball white of "Star" pearl cotton, Article 90, size 5; #7 steel needle; bone ring.

With white, ch 6, join to form a ring, ch 4, * 3 dc in ring, ch 1, repeat from * twice, 2 dc in same space, join in 3rd st of ch. *2nd row:* Ch 1, * 1 sc, ch 3, 1 sc in next ch 1 loop, 2 sc in each of the next 3 dc, repeat from * all around, join in 1st sc. *3rd row:* Ch 3, 2 dc in loop, ch 4, 3 dc in same loop, * ch 3, 3 dc, ch 4, 3 dc in next loop, repeat from * twice, ch 3, join in 3rd st of ch. *4th row:* Ch 3, 2 dc in same space. * ch 3, 3 dc, ch 4, 3 dc in next loop, ch 3, skip 2 dc, 3 dc in next dc, skip the ch 3 loop, 3 dc in next dc, repeat from * all around ending row to correspond, join in

3rd st of ch. *5th row:* Ch 3, 2 dc over same space. * ch 3, dc in next loop, ch 3, 3 dc, ch 5, 3 dc in next loop, ch 3, dc in next loop, ch 3, 3 dc between next two 3 dc groups, repeat from * all around ending row to correspond, join in 3rd st of ch. *6th row:* Sl st to next dc, ch 7, * skip next dc, dc in next dc, ch 4, dc in center dc of next dc group, ch 4, dc in next loop, ch 5, dc in same loop, ch 4, dc in center dc of next dc group, ch 4, dc in next dc, ch 4, dc in center dc of next dc group, ch 4, repeat from * all around ending row to correspond, join. *7th row:* Ch 3, * 4 dc in next loop, dc in next dc, repeat from * twice, 3 dc, ch 3, 3 dc in next loop, dc in next dc, * 4 dc in next loop, dc in next dc, repeat from * once, repeat from 1st * all around ending row to correspond, join. *8th row:* Ch 7, skip 4 dc, dc in next dc, * ch 4, skip 4 dc, dc in next dc, repeat from * once, ch 4, 1 dc, ch 7, 1 dc in next loop, ch 4, skip 3 dc, dc in next dc, * ch 4, skip 4 dc, dc in next dc, repeat from * 3 times, repeat from 1st * all around ending row to correspond, join. *9th row:* Ch 3, * 4 dc in next loop, dc in next dc, repeat from * 3 times, 4 dc, ch 3, 4 dc in next loop, dc in next dc, * 4 dc in next loop, dc in next dc, repeat from * 3 times, repeat from 1st * all around ending row to correspond, join. *10th row:* Ch 7, skip 4 dc, dc in next dc, * ch 4, skip 4 dc, dc in next dc, repeat from * twice, ch 4, dc in next loop, ch 5, dc in same loop. * ch 4, skip 4 dc, dc in next dc, repeat from * 5 times, repeat from 1st * all around ending row to correspond, join. *11th row:* Ch 7, dc in next dc, * ch 4, dc in next dc, repeat from * 3 times, ch 4, 1 dc, ch 5, 1 dc in next loop, * ch 4, dc in next dc, repeat from * 6 times, repeat from 1st * all around ending row to correspond, join. *12th row:* Ch 1 and work 5 sc in each ch 4 loop and 3 sc, ch 3, 3 sc in each corner loop, join, cut thread. *13th row:* Attach color and work

1 sc in each sc and 3 sc in each corner loop, cut thread. Work another section in the same manner.

14th row: Place the 2 sections together having wrong sides facing each other. Attach white in 1st sc of 8th mesh from right-hand corner, working through both sections, work a row of sc all around working 3 sc in corner st to last sc of 8th mesh before same corner (opening for plant), working on remaining back section only, continue in same manner, then work in same manner on remaining front section, join, turn. *15th row:* Working on back section, * ch 5, skip 3 sc, sc in next sc, repeat from * to corner st, ch 7, sc in same space, * ch 5, skip 3 sc, sc in next sc, repeat from * 8 times, then working around lower section, * ch 5, skip 3 sc, sc in next sc, repeat from * to next corner st, continue working in same manner around remaining lower section and front, working all corners same as 1st corner, join, cut thread. *16th row:* Attach color in 1st loop of back section at opening, working around entire outside, omitting front section, work 2 sc, ch 3, 2 sc in each ch 5 loop and 3 sc, ch 3, 3 sc in each corner loop, join in 1st sc. *17th row:* Sl st to next ch 3 loop, * ch 5, sc in next loop, repeat from * to corner loop, ch 7, sc in same loop, continue working all around in same manner working all corners same as 1st corner. *18th row:* Work in same manner as 16th row, join, cut thread. *Next row:* Working in front section only, having wrong side of section toward you, attach color at opening at right-hand side, in each 5 ch loop work, 2 sc, ch 3, 2 sc and 3 sc, ch 3, 3 sc in corner loop, ending row with sl st in opening, turn. *Next row:* Work in same manner as 17th row, ending row with sl st in opening, turn. *Next row:* Work in same manner as 16th row, join, cut thread.

With color, cover a bone ring with sc and sew to holder as illustrated.

Rose Pot Holder

Materials Needed: 1 ball each American Thread Company "Puritan" crochet cotton Article 40 or "De Luxe" crochet cotton Article 346 in cream, kelly green and shaded light pinks *or* "Star" pearl cotton, Article 90, size 5—3 balls cream, 4 balls kelly green, 1 ball shaded pinks; #5 steel needle; bone ring.

For key to abbreviations, see page 128.

Work potholder with a double strand of thread throughout.

With cream, ch 6, join to form a ring, ch 5, dc in ring, * ch 2, dc in ring, repeat from * 5 times, ch 2, join in 3rd st of ch.

2nd row: * Ch 4, sc in next dc, repeat from * all around (8 loops). *3rd row:* Sl st into loop, * ch 7, sc in 2nd st from hook, 1 sdc in each of the next 2 sts of ch (sdc: thread over hook, insert in space, pull through, thread over and work off all loops at one time), 1 dc in each of the next 3 sts of ch, sc in next loop, repeat from * all around. *4th row:* 1 sc in each of the 5 sts on side of petal, 3 sc in point of petal, 5 sc down other side of petal, repeat from beginning all around, join, cut thread. *5th row:* Attach green in point of petal, 3 sc in same space, * 1 sdc in each of the next 2 sc, dc in next sc, thread over hook twice, insert hook in last sc on side of petal and work off 2 loops twice, thread over hook once, insert in 1st sc on side of next petal and work off all loops 2 at a time, skip 2 sc, dc in next sc, 1 sdc in each of the next 2 sc, 3 sc in next sc (top of petal), repeat from * all around in same manner, join. *6th row:* Ch 3, * 3 dc in next sc, 1 dc in each of the next 3 sts, 1 sdc in each of the next 3 sts, 1 dc in each of the next 3 sts, repeat from * all around in same manner, join in 3rd st of ch, cut thread. *7th row:* Attach cream in center st at point, ch 1 and work 3 sc in same space, * 1 sc in each of the next 5 sts, ch 9, 1 sc in 2nd st from hook, 1 sdc in each of the next 3 sts of ch, 1 dc in each of the next 4 sts of ch, skip 1 st of previous row, 1 sc in each of the next 5 sts, 3 sc in next st, repeat from * all around in same manner, join. *8th row:* Ch 1 and work 1 sc in same space, 1 sc in each of the next 6 sc, * skip 1 sc and work 7 sc up side of petal, 3 sc in point of petal, 7 sc down other side of petal, skip 1 sc, 1 sc in each of the next 11 sc, repeat from * all around in same manner ending row with 1 sc in each of the last 4 sc, join, cut thread. *9th row:* Attach green in center st at point of petal and work 3 sc in same space, * sc in next sc, 1 sdc in each of the next 3 sc, dc in next sc, thread over hook twice, skip 2 sc, insert in next sc, pull through, thread over and work off 2 loops twice, thread over hook once, insert in next sc, pull through and work off all loops 2 at a time, skip 2 sc, dc in next sc, sdc in next sc, sc in next sc, sdc in next sc, dc in next sc, skip 2 sc, thread over hook twice, insert in next st, pull through and work off 2 loops twice, thread over hook once, insert in next sc, pull through and work off all loops 2 at a time, skip 2 sc, dc in next sc on side of next petal, 1 sdc in each of the next 3 sc, sc in next sc, 3 sc in next sc, repeat from * all around in same manner, join. *10th row:* Ch 3 and work 3 dc in center st at top of each petal and 1 dc in each remaining st. *11th row:* Ch 3, ** 3 dc in next st (point), 1 dc in each of the next 10 sts, * thread over hook, insert in next st, pull through and work off 2 loops, repeat from * once, thread over and work off all loops at one time (a decrease at base of scallop), 1 dc in each of the next 9 dc, repeat from ** all around in same manner, cut thread.

Work another section in the same manner, and with green, sew the 2 sections together. With green, cover the bone ring with sc and sew to top of holder.

Rose: Using a single strand of thread in shaded pinks, ch 5, join to form a ring, ch 5 dc in ring, * ch 2, dc in ring, repeat from * 3 times, ch 2, join in 3rd st of ch. *Next row:* Sl st into loop, 1 sc, 5 dc, 1 sc in same space, * 1 sc, 5 dc, 1 sc in next loop, repeat from * 4 times, join.

Next row: * Ch 5, sl st in back of work between next 2 petals, repeat from * 5 times.

Next row: Over each loop work 1 sc, 7 dc, 1 sc, join.

Next row: * Ch 7, sl st in back of work, between next 2 petals, repeat from * all around.

Next row: Over each loop work 1 sc, 2 dc, 5 trc, 2 dc, 1 sc, join, cut thread. Sew rose to front of potholder as illustrated.

Corn Pot Holder

Materials Needed: 1 ounce each of American Thread Company "Dawn" knitting worsted, Article W 11 or W 41, in white, amber, and golf green; #7 knitting needles; #4 bone crochet hook.

For key to abbreviations, see page 128.

Starting at lower edge with white, cast on 56 sts and k 1 row. Join amber. *Next row:* * With white, k 7, drop white, pick up amber and k 7, repeat from * across row crossing yarn firmly at back of work.

Next row: * With white, k 7, pass white under needle toward you, then pass amber under needle from you and with amber k 7, repeat from * across row.

Repeat these 2 rows alternating the colors until work measures 8″ from the beginning, bind off, leaving an end. Thread into needle and draw together inserting needle through every 7th st. Work other end in same manner. Sew sides together for 1″ at top and lower end.

Leaves: With green, ch 5, join to form a ring, ch 2, work *

1 sdc in ring (sdc: yarn over hook, insert in ring, pull through, yarn over and work off all loops at one time), ch 18, sl st in 18th st from hook, repeat from * 5 times, join in 2nd st of ch, cut yarn.

Sew to top of holder as illustrated.

Ring: With green, cover a bone ring with sc and attach to top of holder.

And What About Men?

Men are hard to give presents to—everyone says so, so it must be true. But, you know, there are really quite a lot of most acceptable gifts you can whip up for the men in your life if you just put your mind to it. Some men will like any of these things, others may be much more choosy. Knowing your man and his tastes is the keynote, because it's silly to work hard to make something he'll never wear or use!

Shirts

There are more wonderful, gay cottons to be had by the yard for short-sleeved summer sport shirts than one can ever find in ready-made shirts. They aren't very difficult to put together, either, if you sew reasonably well. So consider this the perfect gift for many men. However, if you're not minded to do the whole job from scratch, how about embroidering initials on the pockets of some shirts you buy for your favorite man? It lends a most personal and thoughtful touch, which he'll probably love but would never spend the money on himself.

Other Decorations

Monogrammed handkerchiefs are expensive to buy, but if you'll do the embroidery yourself, much will be saved and the gift far more endearing because your own hands have made it special. Then, there's an amusing and fine thing you can do, and if your man has a sense of humor (which we sincerely hope!), he will love this present best of all. Chain stitch "Happy Easter" on those shorts he's needed and kept forgetting to buy!

Gloves

So few men *ever* wear gloves today that they should be presented only to one you know will want them. However, if yours is that meticulous a dresser, why not whip him up a pair of string gloves? They're very smart for spring wear and the right man will be delighted with such a gift.

Scarves

Far more men wear scarves than wear gloves. The best kind to make for a man is a double-thickness silk one—either with both sides of the same pattern, both sides plain, or one plain and the other figured. Then, many men like to wear scarves tucked into the necks of sports shirts in summer. These are best in single thickness and may be either silk or cotton. They should, of course, be made shorter by far than the kind he'd like to wear under his coat in chilly weather.

For the Golfer

There's no present more acceptable to a golfing man than new golf balls. Why not let the children make him a lovely Easter basket—and have the "eggs" be golf balls?

Really Personal

If you have children, take some brand new, delightful pictures of them and then let them make a picture album for Daddy, cutting its pages in egg-shape from heavy paper. Both givers and receivers will get a big thrill out of this.

Crocheted Necktie
(Plate 34)

Materials Needed: 2 balls (any color you choose) American Thread Company "Puritan" crochet cotton, Article 40 or "De Luxe" crochet cotton, Article 346, or 4 balls "Star" pearl cotton, Article 90, size 5; #10 steel needle; ¼ yard of ½″ ribbon.
For key to abbreviations, see page 128.

PLATE 34
CROCHETED NECKTIE

Gauge: 2 shells equals 2″.

Tie should be worked *firmly*.

Ch 25, 3 dc in 5th st from hook, skip 3 sts of ch, sc in next st, * ch 2, 3 dc in same space, skip 3 sts of ch, sc in next st, repeat from * 3 times (5 shells), ch 4, turn. *2nd row:* 3 dc in same space, * sc in ch 2 loop of next shell, ch 2, 3 dc in same space (pattern), repeat from * 3 times, sc in ch 2 loop of last shell, ch 4, turn. Repeat 2nd row until work measures 16″ from beginning, ch 4, turn. *Next row:* 3 dc in same space, sc in ch 2 loop of next shell, pull loop through, repeat from * once, thread over hook and pull through all 3 loops at one time (a decrease of 1 shell), ch 2, 3 dc in same space, sc in ch 2 loop of next shell, ch 2, 3 dc in same space, sc in ch 2 loop of last shell, ch 4, turn (4 shells). Work even in pattern for 2½″, ch 4, turn.

Next row: 3 dc in same space, sc in ch 2 loop of next shell, ch 2, 3 dc in same space, dec in next 2 shells, ch 2, 3 dc in same space, sc in ch 2 loop of last shell, ch 4, turn (3 shells). Work even in pattern until tie measures 21″, ch 1, turn.

Next row (Neckband): Sc in next sc, * 1 sc in each 3 dc of next shell, repeat from * twice, sc in ch 2 loop of last shell, ch 1, turn (11 sc).

Next row: 1 sc in each sc, ch 1, turn. Repeat last row until band measures 12″, ch 4, turn. *Next row:* 3 dc in same space, skip next 3 sts, sc in next st, ch 3, 2 dc in same space, skip next 2 sts, sc in next st, ch 2, 3 dc in same space, skip next 2 sts, sc in last st, ch 4, turn (3 shells). Work even in pattern for 2½″, ch 4, turn.

Next row: 3 dc in same space, sc in ch 2 loop of next shell, ch 2, 3 dc in same space, sc in next sc between shells, ch 2, 3 dc in same space, sc in ch 2 loop of next shell, ch 2, 3 dc in same space, sc in ch 2 loop of last shell, ch 4, turn (4 shells). Work even in pattern for 10½″, cut yarn. Face neckband with ribbon.

Socks

There probably couldn't be a much more universally acceptable present for men than hand-knitted socks. If your man is the argyle type, you can get all the equipment and instructions neatly done up in a little kit almost anywhere you go looking for it. I give you here, however, a slightly more unusual, though thoroughly conservative, sock which I think you'll find fun to make.

Cable Socks

Materials Needed: 2 2-ounce skeins "Botany" terratones; 1 set #1 d.p. needles (Standard); 1 set #4 d.p. needles (Standard); 1 tapestry needle.

For key to abbreviations, see page 128.

Gauge: 7 sts to 1″; 9 rows to 1″.

Leg: With #1 d.p. needles, cast on 60 sts. Divide evenly on 3 needles. Join, being careful not to twist. K 2, p 2 in ribbing for 36 rows, change to #4 d.p. needles and work pattern as follows:

1st row: K 2, p 2, k 6, p 2, k 20, p 2, k 6, p 2, k 18. *2nd row:* K 2, * p 2, slip next 3 sts to cable needle and hold in front of work, k next 3 sts, k 3 sts from cable needle, p 2, * k 20, repeat between * s, k 18. *3rd, 4th, 5th, and 6th rows:* Same as 1st row. Repeat these 6 rows until sock measures 11″ from start or desired length to heel. Place 30 sts on 2 needles for instep, including 3 sts of cable at each end. On remaining 30 sts, k 1 row, p 1 row for 2″. Turn heel as follows: Starting on a p row, p 17, p 2 tog, p 1, turn. Sl 1, k 5, sl 1, k 1, psso, k 1, turn. Sl 1, p 6, p 2 tog, p 1, turn. Sl 1, k 7, sl 1, k 1, psso, k 1, turn. Sl 1, p 8, p 2 tog, p 1, turn. Continue in this manner, working 1 st more each row until all sts have been worked: 18 sts on needle.

Place 9 sts on each of 2 needles. Keeping 9 sts on needle, pick up 13 sts along side of heel (first needle—22 sts). Work in pattern across instep sts (second needle—30 sts). Pick up 13 sts along other side of heel and k 9 sts onto same needle (third needle—22 sts).

Gusset: Shape as follows: *1st row:* * K to last 3 sts of first needle, k 2 tog, k 1; work in pattern across second needle; k 1, sl 1, k 1, psso, k to end of third needle. *2nd row:* Knit. Repeat these 2 rows until there are 15 sts on both the first and third needles. Work even keeping the instep sts in pattern until foot measures 2″ less than desired length from back of heel. For example: 8″ for size 10; 9″ for size 11; 10″ for size 12.

Toe: Shape as follows: * K to last 2 sts of first needle, k 2 tog, k 1, k 1, sl 1, k 1, psso, k to last 3 sts of second needle, k 2 tog, k 1, k 1, sl 1, k 1, psso, k to end of 3rd needle. Work 1 rnd even. Repeat from * until 6 sts remain on second needle and 3 sts each on first and 3rd needles. Weave sts tog.

13

Easter Cards and Easter Plants

There is an Easter card to fit every taste, mood, and age level to be bought in the stationery, gift, and department stores of this country. Some cling closely to the religious tradition, some feature bunnies and chicks and flowers, while some are comic. Your background and your own feeling for the season will dictate the kind you choose, and I feel that advice from me on their purchase is utterly superfluous. Still, I can suggest that you tuck a dainty, springlike handkerchief or a sachet or a dollar bill for a young 'un into the cards you send to special people. To someone far away and dear to you, you might enclose a sheet of stamps, unless you think that's too much of a hint!

If you can, choose cards with room for you to write your own message, however small, and however much you may like the printed one. Easter is one of those heart-warming times when it's the *personal* feeling you have that gets over and matters to the people who love you. The thoughtfulness of sending a card is *almost* enough. Your own message is the perfect supplement.

The most endearing cards at Easter or any other season are the ones made right from the start by children. All they need is good strong paper to cut and fold, crayons or water colors, and their own lively and charming imaginations. If your children yearn to do a more elaborate job than these simple ingredients would allow, give them also glue or rubber cement and little bits of feathers, cotton, sequins, packaged glitter, lace-paper doilies, and green shredded cellophane—and watch them produce!

As always, if you want your children to achieve the greatest potential of which they are capable in any field, do not proffer advice or do their jobs for them. Be handy by to offer advice and help *if it's requested*. Keep firmly in mind the natural difference between the standards of your age and theirs. They will never achieve yours without embarrassment and heartbreak (and perhaps never at all), if they realize that you are making fun or deprecating their efforts. Your interest is what they need and want—and a judicious bit of praise, too. But don't even overdo that. Children are wise, and inclined to be honest with themselves. It's fine to be reassured, but overpraise is just discomforting!

Easter Plants

Easter is the time of year when it is most customary to give plants to one's friends. They somehow epitomize the spirit of the season. They are the symbol of bursting-forth from the dreary, dark days into flower and the promise of foliage. Their care is most important, as many desperately "brown-thumbed" people know to their sorrow. Having been one of those people myself, my sympathy is great and my message is heartening!

First, I discovered that many plants, like ivy and philodendron, for instance, love to be treated quite roughly. I think that statement can be made about any of the plants whose leaves like to be watered. Don't just dribble water on them, give them a good *hard* spraying. And don't do it too often. It's easy to talk about watering plants when "the soil feels dry," but a brown thumb can't tell when that is, even though the green one thinks it's simple. I have found that there's less danger of ruining house plants by healthy neglect than by coddling.

The plants most commonly given at Easter time are hydrangeas, azaleas, hyacinths, lilies, daphnes, and gardenias.

It's especially nice to give plants which can be permanently transplanted to the outdoors if the people to whom you give them have gardens. My mother, for example, has the most wonderful collection of huge azalea and hydrangea bushes, all of which started as Easter plants, and about each of which, by the way, she can tell you the exact history and include the name of the donor! There could be no more lasting gift.

For friends who live in city apartments or houses, choose any plant which can be kept going in the proper window and with the proper care. With which, let us discuss care of the plants previously mentioned. One of the best aids I've had is *Enjoy Your House Plants* by Dorothy Jenkins and Helen Van Pelt Wilson (M. Barrows & Co. Inc., $3.00). It is a wonderfully simple, helpful, and engaging book.

Hydrangeas

First, while they're in the house, keep them in a light window. If there are buds to open, plants must have some sun; otherwise in-bloom plants last longer just in the light. Hydrangeas are exceedingly thirsty, so will do best if they're watered every day. They're always in bloom when they arrive as an Easter present, and you can keep them looking pretty and blooming until time to put them out in the garden if you give them enough to drink. It is sometimes necessary to water twice a day. In some cold sections, hydrangeas which have been forced are not likely to survive if planted in the ground, so be sure to ascertain, if you can, whether yours can take it. We've had very good luck planting them outdoors in northern New Jersey.

If you're considering keeping an Easter hydrangea as a house plant, realize, please, that they grow like mad and are likely to need repotting fairly frequently, which is a nuisance. Besides that, when the plant reaches a size requiring a tub the average small apartment won't hold it. However, if you intend to keep it inside, at least for one extra winter, try to put it outdoors with its pot plunged in the ground during the summer. Water it frequently. And feed it with liquid manure from August on (about twice a month). In October, the plant should be retired to a cold, but not freezing, place for a rest. It is kept thus until January, with once-a-week-watering and then brought out into a south window to get started on looking like an Easter present for the second time!

Azaleas

Azaleas like full sun in the house for four or five hours a day. I hope, if you receive lots of these and hydrangeas, that you have lots of southern exposure! But the azaleas can do in an east or west window. Put the pot into a deep bowl or saucer and keep it filled with water, watering at least once a day. Exception —once a week let it get dryish and then immerse the whole pot to within an inch of the top in a pail or sink and let it stay there until the soil has drawn up enough water to be really wet. Be sure to nip off all faded blooms, which is something to remember about any plant, because those wilted bits just sap strength.

There are some azaleas which are too tender to be transplanted to the garden. Try to discover whether yours is one of this kind. If it is, repot it in fresh soil with broken pot or pebbles in the bottom for drainage, and plunge the pot into the garden soil in a partially shaded spot. Azaleas continue to need lots of water when they're summering in the garden. They also like a bit of feeding, at perhaps six-week intervals. When they are brought indoors again before frost, they take their resting period. At this point they should not be fed, but they do need water—not as much as when they're blooming, but they shouldn't dry out. They like light, not full sun, at this period, and should be cool. In November, they can be transferred to a south window, fed weekly, and watered often. When they begin to bloom, put them into an east or west window.

Hyacinths

These should be watered about three times a week while they're blooming—and they do exceedingly well outdoors if you take proper care of them between flowering in the house and planting time in the fall. When the blooms die, cut them off, then continue to water the plants as needed until the leaves begin to turn yellow. Now the bulbs are ready to rest. Store them in their pots in a cool, dry place. Along about June, take them out of the pots to dry out. Then plant them in the garden in the fall.

Lilies

Give your Easter lilies plenty of water and keep them in sunlight if there are buds to open, otherwise a light place is preferable. A feeding every two weeks will help. They cannot be grown outside north of Washington, D.C., but if you take proper care of them during the Easter season and then set them out in the garden they *may* bloom again that summer.

Daphne

These pretty, sweet-scented plants like sun. They also require careful watering and should never be allowed to go dry, though every-other-day may be often enough. They do nicely planted in the garden permanently in a good, sunny spot.

Gardenias

These are a rather expensive Easter present, but frequently given. Even a truly green-thumb gardener may well grit his teeth at the thought of trying to keep a gardenia plant going out of its native southern habitat. Sometimes it does.

Gardenias love to have their leaves sprayed gently with water. If you really want to keep yours going, you'll give it this treatment every day, though once a week *may* be enough. It also likes to sit in a saucer or bowl of water and to be immersed to within an inch of the top of the pot once a week. Gardenias like sun in the morning, but after their leaves have been sprayed, they should not be put back into the sun until they are entirely dry.

Unless a gardenia plant is quite evidently taking a rest and shows no sign of new growth, it should be fed about once a month. If you have one of the rare ones which doesn't collapse completely within a month or two of Easter day, sit it outside in a fairly shady (not deep shade), place for the summer, watering it frequently, and watching carefully for mealy bug or red spider, which may attack it. These must be got rid of at once, the mealy bug by means of a cotton-wrapped toothpick dipped in alcohol, and the red spider by means of a hearty spraying with cold water. A plant which was covered with blossoms at Easter may be equally covered three months later!

Bulbs to Grow Yourself

Even though florist's plants are beautiful and make wonderful gifts for anyone, you may prefer to add your own truly personal touch by growing some bulbs which you will present to friends. Narcissus, Dutch, Roman, or grape hyacinths, or daffodils are quite easy to handle indoors yourself and make lovely presents for your friends.

Forced Branches

Of course, it depends partly upon the part of the country from which you come and partly upon the date of Easter in any particular year, but if you plan cannily in advance you may be able to force forsythia, pussy willows, lilacs, peach, pear, apple, cherry, or crab-apple blossoms for the Easter season—given that the circumstances don't provide them to you out of doors. You can make lovely arrangements with them—and an inexpensive, but beautiful, container to hold them makes the gift permanent.

To force branches, cut them as soon as there is slightest sign of buds. Bring them into the house and put them in water.

Index